Cambridge Elements

Elements in Cognitive Linguistics
edited by
Sarah Duffy
Northumbria University
Nick Riches
Newcastle University

APPLIED COGNITIVE LINGUISTICS AND L2 INSTRUCTION

Reyes Llopis-García
Columbia University

CAMBRIDGE
UNIVERSITY PRESS

Shaftesbury Road, Cambridge CB2 8EA, United Kingdom

One Liberty Plaza, 20th Floor, New York, NY 10006, USA

477 Williamstown Road, Port Melbourne, VIC 3207, Australia

314–321, 3rd Floor, Plot 3, Splendor Forum, Jasola District Centre,
New Delhi – 110025, India

103 Penang Road, #05–06/07, Visioncrest Commercial, Singapore 238467

Cambridge University Press is part of Cambridge University Press & Assessment,
a department of the University of Cambridge.

We share the University's mission to contribute to society through the pursuit of
education, learning and research at the highest international levels of excellence.

www.cambridge.org
Information on this title: www.cambridge.org/9781009468282

DOI: 10.1017/9781009128094

© Reyes Llopis-García 2024

This publication is in copyright. Subject to statutory exception and to the provisions
of relevant collective licensing agreements, no reproduction of any part may take
place without the written permission of Cambridge University Press & Assessment.

First published 2024

A catalogue record for this publication is available from the British Library

ISBN 978-1-009-46828-2 Hardback
ISBN 978-1-009-12431-7 Paperback
ISSN 2633-3325 (online)
ISSN 2633-3317 (print)

Cambridge University Press & Assessment has no responsibility for the persistence
or accuracy of URLs for external or third-party internet websites referred to in this
publication and does not guarantee that any content on such websites is, or will
remain, accurate or appropriate.

Applied Cognitive Linguistics and L2 Instruction

Elements in Cognitive Linguistics

DOI: 10.1017/9781009128094
First published online: February 2024

Reyes Llopis-García
Columbia University

Author for correspondence: Reyes Llopis-García, rl2506@columbia.edu

Abstract: Both applied cognitive linguistics (ACL) researchers and linguists, and language instructors and professionals looking for a comprehensive and innovative access to ACL from the direct point of view of applied L2 Pedagogy, will find this Element to be of interest. There is great demand for quality teaching materials, a need for guidance on how to design them and which technology tools are of value. This Element takes a theoretical approach to that design while offering direct examples and tips for practitioners and researchers. Questions about empirical studies are explored, probing prominent empirical research, and the author provides promising evidence to support their recommendations on assessment-task design for future research. Linguists, researchers, linguistics students, graduate academic programs, and teachers of L2 languages alike will find value in this Element.

Keywords: cognitive linguistics, L2 pedagogy, L2 instruction, assessment design, second language acquisition

ISBNs: 9781009468282 (HB), 9781009124317 (PB), 9781009128094 (OC)
ISSNs: 2633-3325 (online), 2633-3317 (print)

Contents

Introduction

The last twenty years have seen a prolific rise in research and publications in the intersection of cognitive linguistics (CL) and L2[1] pedagogy, now known as applied cognitive linguistics (ACL), and the conversation so far has been enriching and productive. Although the end of the 1990s saw some promising publications in the field (Boers & Demecheleer 1998; Deignan, Gabrys, & Solska 1997; Kövecses & Szabó 1996, to name a few), it was with the publication of the two volumes by Pütz, Niemeier, and Dirven (2001a; 2001b) that the field of ACL emerged as a discipline for the study of acquisition processes and approaches to L2 pedagogy, considering them complementary and not antagonistic, and thus rejecting the (still relevant today) learning versus acquisition dichotomy proposed by Krashen (1985).

Achard and Niemeier (2004) followed up shortly after with another edited volume on the topic and Boers and Lindstromberg (2008) focused on ACL and vocabulary. After Robinson and Ellis (2008) edited the *Handbook of Cognitive Linguistics and Second Language Acquisition*, offering valuable insight into the theoretical foundations and potential of ACL, De Knop, Boers, and De Rycker (2010) went further in a much-needed specific direction: L2 language teaching and ACL, arguing that instruction that draws inspiration from this intersection "can help improve efficient use of those interventions through their capacity to forge robust form-meaning mappings in memory" (p. 15). Their volume included studies with results that signaled advisable directions in which to teach vocabulary, grammatical items, constructions, and even pronunciation. All contributions strongly recommended teacher interventions and explanations, and advocated for the great potential of ACL-trained instructors (and not just as researchers collecting data). The same year, Littlemore and Juchem-Grundmann (2010) published a Special Issue that further reinforced the call for more ACL applications in language teaching, and that also included studies with successful data from classroom instruction (Llopis-García 2010 for Spanish/L2 and Tyler, Mueller, & Ho 2010 for English/L2).

For the case of English as a foreign language (EFL), Tyler (2012) laid out the theoretical groundwork of ACL in its intersection with EFL learning and offered promising results from classroom-based studies on prepositions, modal verbs, and constructions. Bielak and Pawlak (2013) did the same and focused on tense and aspect. To date, these volumes, especially the first one, might be the most comprehensive and accessible

---

[1] For the sake of coherence, the term L2 will refer to second and foreign language learning, as well as to the more recent "world/global language" designation, which seeks to dispense with potentially negative connotations associated with the "foreign" label.

guides for English-speaking instructors seeking professional development and an academic approach to ACL.

For the pedagogy of languages other than English, the Special Issue on *Applied Cognitive Linguistics to L2 Acquisition and Learning* (Llopis-García & Hijazo-Gascón 2019) also included empirical classroom data (Colasacco 2019), along with other studies seeking to offer pedagogical considerations and renewing the call for ACL teaching materials. The same year also brought the eagerly-awaited edited volume on *Cognitive Linguistics and Spanish L2/FL* (Ibarretxe-Antuñano, Cadierno, & Castañeda Castro 2019), featuring empirical and theoretical approaches to Spanish grammatical features (such as articles, the verbal system, mood selection, comparative constructions, prepositions, and metaphors), all revisited from a CL lens.

All works cited in this literature review present a wide-ranging panorama of the field, and even include studies that have been successful at operating with CL-based principles in the actual language classroom. But questions remain:

(1) Why are there not *more* classroom-based studies that provide solid evidence that ACL instruction for grammar and lexis is superior to current methodologies that draw on notional-functional approaches? How is it possible that with so many encouraging works aimed at proving the successful allyship of ACL and L2 teaching, after twenty plus years there is still no consistent and definite evidence that *it really works in the classroom*? Sections 4 and 5 address this issue and introduce studies and works that deal with research in the L2 classroom.

(2) Why are there not *more* examples of ACL teaching materials? How can instructors create their own materials or publishers bring ACL ideas into textbooks if there are no concrete examples or explanations on how to design and develop content? Section 4 is entirely devoted to teaching materials, including published works that offer pedagogical proposals.

(3) Who is learning about CL outside of the realm of linguistics and how, if at all, are L2 instructors accessing the ideas and potential of ACL for their language classrooms? There seems to be an undeniable gap between academic scholarship and L2 language instruction (which includes instructors, textbook publishers, and material designers), two fields often intertwined, as the literature above aptly shows, but hardly ever truly merged for lasting impact in the language classroom.

This Element seeks to answer these questions from an applied and pedagogical perspective. The aim is to show that *there is already* ample work being done in the ACL-based L2 classroom and that the prospects are encouraging. But also, that there is room *and need* for more: more collaborations between instructors and researchers; more professional development for instructors on ACL and for researchers on pedagogy; and more examples of teaching materials and classroom content that can serve as stepping stones for others to design their own. The perspective offered in this Element seeks to truly integrate both fields through *the experience of the ACL classroom itself.*[2]

To this end, Section 1 will explain how the grammar-lexis continuum is addressed in current market-ready textbooks and will offer a general overview of the issues that separate language teaching from linguistics. Sections 2, 3, and 4 will endeavor to show not only that ACL has great classroom potential but, rather, that the principles that inform ACL *are present* in the lessons that are *already being taught* by language instructors themselves. To that end, Section 2 presents the main concepts from ACL and how they relate to teaching. Section 3 addresses ACL instruction with the solid allyship of contributions from second language acquisition (SLA) (focus on form for grammar and lexical approaches for vocabulary). Section 4 dives deeper into pedagogical design, especially from the lens of the contributions that educational technology can offer ACL content design (and especially since the COVID-19 pandemic has forced many L2 instructors to teach and find resources online). Section 5 will depart from teaching and focus on the empirical challenges of proving the efficacy of ACL in the L2 classroom. This section will also address the reasons why I think that research has not been able to deliver the expected results and will present an empirical study that does, thereby offering new avenues for research and testing. Section 6 gathers the main ideas from this Element and serves as a closing statement.

1 L2 Language Teaching versus the Linguistics of L2

It is a truth universally acknowledged that L2 language teaching, if it aims to be truly enriching for students, must be in need of constant revision and update, and its instructors must be in continuous professional development in order to be able to understand and apply new approaches.

This Jane Austen freestyle seems sensible, but the actual truth is that this is all harder than it seems. On the one hand, it is accurate to say that there is a significant correspondence between research in theoretical fields such as SLA and real-life applications that have made a difference in L2 instruction. On the other hand, a great deal of past and current research never reaches the pedagogical practice of the classroom. This is so because: (a) SLA publications stay within the field and

---

[2] The examples provided will largely be from the Spanish/L2 classroom and will endeavor to serve as a template for other languages, thus contributing to advancing the visibility and potential of ACL beyond the English language proposed by Hijazo-Gascón & Llopis-García (2019). Readers of this Element are hereby invited and encouraged to use all materials proposed here for their own teaching practice or research.

do not reach the teaching community or the textbook publishing industry; (b) research and insights into acquisition and learning are slow to find their way to the professional and academic development of instructors; and (c) because research is too theoretical or too challenging to translate into best pedagogical practices that may be of immediate interest to L2 instructors. There is a (d) to this issue, and it is the disconnect that exists between linguists and language instructors, easily verifiable from the fact that there are very few academic spaces that bring the two communities together and that enable or foster their collaborations and interactions. This last point has a very real impact (although it is highly underrated) in the research that linguists conduct in the L2 classroom. Section 5 on cognitive empirical design will speak to this issue in depth.

As Larsen-Freeman exemplifies when reviewing literature on different instructional practices, "SLA researchers often seek to define what is minimally necessary to explain language acquisition. What is minimally needed is not necessarily what is optimal for classroom instruction" (2015: 266). In this breach between research and language teaching, if the experience of a researcher in the language classroom is limited to the temporary presence of an empirical study, language instructors could rightly point out that their understanding of what happens in the classroom is insufficient and incomplete. However, when teachers plan their lessons, the highly theoretical and often hard-to-access literature from linguistics is not first and foremost on their to-do list. These are professionals who teach and grade every day, prepare and impart lessons, find alternative materials (because textbooks are often not helpful enough), give feedback, and deal with service to their schools, departments, or universities. In the experience of teachers, and as Toth and Davin (2016: 151) state: "Every calculation of what to do in the classroom, and when or how, is a function of how much time we have, and it is perhaps because time is so deeply embedded in our experience of learning that L2 theories have not recognized more overtly how essential time management is to pedagogical effectiveness."

1.1 The Specific Case of Applied Cognitive Linguistics (ACL)

Cognitive linguistics (CL) and all related disciplines view language as a general, integrated part of human cognition that emerges from our physical, sensorimotor and bodily experiences, as well as from our interaction with the world around (Lakoff & Johnson 1980; Langacker 1987, 2009, and 2016; Kövecses 2002; Robinson & Ellis 2008; Ibarretxe-Antuñano & Valenzuela 2012, Littlemore & Taylor 2014; Tyler, Huang, & Jan 2018). Other foundational ideas that will be addressed throughout this volume describe language as symbolic, embodied, motivated, and usage-based.

For the case of L2 pedagogy, Langacker himself, back in 2008, recognized that the impact of linguists on real, day-to-day L2 language instruction had a lot to be desired, and added that it had, in fact, "been less than miraculous and sometimes less than helpful" (2008a: 66). This distance between research and pedagogy is widely recognized in the field (Achard 2008; Littlemore 2009; Llopis-García 2011; Tyler 2012; Suñer & Roche 2019; Piquer-Píriz & Alejo-González 2020), and turns the lack of materials that are informed by linguistic theory into "a hunt" that keeps ACL content away from the mainstream L2 classroom (Nacey 2017: 511). Piquer-Píriz (2021) also points out that although ACL-based materials are very attractive "on paper," there are three main caveats to their design: (a) it takes time to develop them at home and time to implement them in class and, usually, availability of time when there is a curriculum to cover is a scarce commodity; (b) they require training and know-how, especially when quality professional development may be difficult to come by beyond regular work hours; and (c) guidelines and directives to work with these materials are not present in the descriptors of either the Common European Reference Framework (CERF 2001)[3] or the American Council for the Teaching of Foreign Languages (ACTFL),[4] greatly hindering their mainstream availability.

But the potential is unequivocal. And one important aspect of ACL for L2 is the difference between grammar and vocabulary or, rather, the lack thereof. In the words of Langacker on the architecture of cognitive grammar, "lexicon, morphology and syntax form a continuum" (2009: 1). This idea is radically different from more traditional approaches to language and linguistics, such as generative linguistics (as well as general methodological approaches to L2), where all three components are studied and understood as separate entities. Langacker goes on to say that CL "claims that lexicon and grammar are fully describable as assemblies of symbolic structures, where a symbolic structure is simply the pairing between a semantic structure and a phonological structure" (p. 1). These structures, also known as *constructions*, may be formed by one or many words and acquire their status by having both grammatical structure (schematic in nature) and semantic value. The combination of both is what guarantees their (phonological) presence in the linguistic repertoire of a language. As Holme (2010a: 120) states, "teaching language content does not mean emphasizing grammar over lexis or lexis over grammar. Rather it is a case of taking up different positions along the lexico-grammatical continuum."

Construction grammar (Goldberg 1995, 2003), another discipline within CL, also "considers that all grammatical phenomena can be understood as learned

[3] www.coe.int/en/web/common-european-framework-reference-languages
[4] www.actfl.org/

pairings of form [and meaning], which applies to all range of linguistic items, from morphemes to idioms" (Hijazo-Gascón & Llopis-García 2019: 5). And since all these items have semantic value, the continuum between grammar and vocabulary is upheld.

For cognitive linguists, then, grammar and lexis are one and the same, and this fundamental consideration has very interesting implications for the teaching and learning of L2s. It can all start with a challenge to the structure of most market-ready textbooks, where the notional-functional division of chapters (see Section 1.2.1) presents the vocabulary, the grammatical structures, and the pragmatic/contextual information as separate segments within each.

1.2 Aspects of Grammar and Vocabulary in Current L2 Methods

Larsen-Freeman (2015) pointed out that "grammar instruction has been relatively unaltered by research findings. It remains traditional for the most part, with grammar teaching centered on accuracy of form and rule learning, and with mechanical exercises seen as the way to bring about the learning of grammar" (p. 263). And she is not the only one. Lee & VanPatten, back in 2003, observed that many of the important issues about teaching grammar communicatively (i.e., teaching language in ways that are engaging and meaningful for use in real-life social interactions beyond the classroom, as opposed to studying the grammatical system from a theoretical perspective) "seem to be ignored" in most textbooks available in the market (2003: 1). And Tyler (2012), when addressing L2 teaching methodologies (mostly for English as L2, but with clear generalization value), remarks that across time, "while the approaches have changed, the view of the nature and structure of language that underpins these approaches has not. What is remarkable is that the pedagogical grammar adopted by all these approaches is strikingly similar and has changed very little over the past 70 years" (p. 7). This is what Llopis-García, Real Espinosa, and Ruiz Campillo (2012: 10) call the "methodological fallacy," whereby there is a belief that grammar will be successfully taught when integrated in the methodology *du jour* because *this time*, it will provide better understanding and use for the students.

There are directions in the literature on L2 pedagogy and SLA of when to teach grammar, how much to teach, and how to do it. What there is less of, however, is *what kind of grammar should be taught*. As Méndez Santos and Llopis-García (2021: 262. OT[5]) point out, the grammar-translation

---

[5] This acronym will refer to my own translation, that is, direct quotes that I have translated from their original language into English.

method[6] and the structuralist perspective on language are still present in many classrooms and textbooks. This hinges on lack of resources, institutional decisions, and sometimes on tradition and beliefs about what learning a language implies.

These unchanging conditions maintain the status quo because grammar, regardless of any state-of-the-art methodology, largely: (a) follows a notional-functional approach (see Section 1.2.1); (b) is understood as an object of study; and (c) is still the apple of discord in L2 teaching. Let us consider all these aspects individually.

1.2.1 Grammar Follows a Notional-Functional Approach

The introduction of grammar in the classroom is usually dictated by the textbook content, and most textbooks are organized by chapters or units with a topic to cover. Organizing a syllabus or a textbook around "notions" or real-life situations, and then selecting the linguistic structures or "functions" used to communicate them, is what drives the notional-functional approach.

For a B1 level of Spanish, for instance, and following the descriptors of the *Plan Curricular del Instituto Cervantes* (PCIC, Curriculum Plan of the Cervantes Institute 2006),[7] topics include: *telling personal anecdotes in the past; talking about future plans, hypothesis, and conditions;* and *expressing opinions, agreement, and disagreement*, etc. Grammatical content, then, follows the demands of the communicative needs of the unit in question and is learned "at a local level," instead of holistically or with a more global perspective to account for polysemy, multiple usages, or different contextual cues.

Around since the early 1970s, grammatical content in most available textbooks still follows a notional-functional approach, even if the overall methodology is framed as action-oriented, content-based, blended learning, or project-based learning (to name a few currently popular teaching methods that do not extend their innovations to their treatment of grammar). According to this approach, language conveys meaning, but it needs a situational context of use to acquire "communicative value." By this view, when performing "communicative acts", there are "functions of language" as communicative categories (*giving advice, addressing a letter, introducing oneself . . .*) that must be paired vis-à-vis linguistic "notions" (*the conditional, greetings and salutations, reflexive verbs . . .*) (Littlewood 2011).

---

[6] A teaching methodology popular in the late nineteenth century that studied language via contrastive translation of examples from the L2 to the students' L1. It also structured language practice with a focus on forms over meaning.

[7] https://cvc.cervantes.es/ensenanza/biblioteca_ele/plan_curricular/

This is especially true for the triple breakdown of the Spanish verbal system, where tenses are introduced according to three dimensions. The first one is *linguistic form* (i.e. "the imperfect future tense," built with the infinitive and the added endings *-é, -ás, -á, -emos, -éis, -án* for all three conjugations); the second one is *meaning* (i.e. "it is a simple tense to talk about actions in the future"); and the third one is *use* (i.e. to name a few: *predictions, projections, promises, resolutions, future actions, to reassure someone about something, to express uncertainty in the present . . .*). When a verbal tense is presented in this manner in textbooks, the uses are not taught together. Instead, they are spread out across chapters and thematic units, dependent on contextual cues and pragmatic scenarios.

Another example of this practice relates to the presentation of the so-called "conditional" tense in Spanish. In elementary levels (such as A2 of the PCIC, although it does not appear explicitly in the descriptors[8] of the level), the tense is briefly first learned to "express wishes" and is taught mostly as a chunk (*me gustaría* [*I would like*] + infinitive). As students progress on to the B1 level,[9] the conditional adds "courtesy and modesty" to its usage range (*¿Podría hablar con usted?* [*could I speak with you?*]), mostly to give advice (*Yo en tu lugar, iría al médico* [*In your place, I would go to the doctor*]). It is also studied when addressing indirect speech, that is, to refer to the words of another in the past (*Iré a la fiesta → ella dijo que iría a la fiesta* [*I will go to the party → she said she would go to the party*]). Well into the B2 level,[10] the descriptor is "probability in the past." This is the first time that students ever learn that the conditional is a past tense: "expressing posteriority to another event in the past (*consecutio temporum*)," "conditional sentences with the imperfect subjunctive" (*Si pudiera, iría a la fiesta* [*If I could, I would go to the party*]), or to "express hypothetical wishes" (*Me comería una pizza* [*I could eat some pizza*]). In the C1–C2 levels,[11] the tense is taught to "object to or reject something in the past" (*Sería muy listo, pero . . .* [*he may be really smart, but . . .*]), or to "warn/express fear in the past," among other highly context-dependent uses.

Such a scattered view of this tense (Llopis-García 2016a),[12] peppered over levels and class sessions, effectively disconnects both instructors and learners

---

[8] https://cvc.cervantes.es/ensenanza/biblioteca_ele/plan_curricular/niveles/02_gramatica_inventario_a1-a2.htm
[9] https://cvc.cervantes.es/ensenanza/biblioteca_ele/plan_curricular/niveles/02_gramatica_inventario_b1-b2.htm
[10] https://cvc.cervantes.es/ensenanza/biblioteca_ele/plan_curricular/niveles/02_gramatica_inventario_b1-b2.htm
[11] https://cvc.cervantes.es/ensenanza/biblioteca_ele/plan_curricular/niveles/02_gramatica_inventario_c1-c2.htm
[12] www.youtube.com/watch?v=ngkUwCpacdw

from a holistic understanding, and forces them to learn on a need-to-know basis across textbook units and competence levels. However, if a grammar approach is meant to truly be useful in the L2 classroom, it will be because it is able to replicate "a model of language manipulation capable of explaining and generating the same effects of communication and meaning that we can observe in real use" (Llopis-García et al. 2012: 20. OT).

1.2.2 Grammar Is Understood as an Object of Study

Despite claims of "communicative purposes," L2 grammar is still largely studied as a "foreign object," by itself and without the input of the L1s or other languages that the students may know. Without interlinguistic reflection and *motivation*[13] as a way to understand its constructional and semantic value, the grammar charts and tables at the end of every unit in the textbook become stand-alone items of study and memorization through practice exercises. As Toth and Davin point out, "metalinguistic information and feedback intended to foster L2 accuracy must be refined and strategically provided as essential supports for meaningful communication, rather than as ends unto themselves" (2016: 152).

Despite ubiquitous talks of "communicative" grammar, what we find in most L2 textbooks is unquestionably "foreign," full of rules, exceptions, and opaque metalanguage. There is no space for the students' L1, so interlinguistic reflections and introspectiveness about "why we say what we say" are not a fostered classroom dynamic and do not become part of the students' learning process. Many language instructors might recognize the moment of *"Okay, time for some grammar now!"* during their lesson and know that this is inevitably accompanied by groans from the students and promises of "more fun" times ahead, like a song or a role-play activity.

Instruction that presents linguistic forms as a result of the (foreign) system, subordinate to rules and exceptions over which the learner has no control and must be learned "as is" stands to bore, demotivate, and disenfranchise learners from their goals of fluency. When treating grammar as an object of study in the classroom, the PPP (presentation-practice-production) method inevitably appears: *Presentation* of new grammar – where the instructor introduces, explains, and exemplifies the target structure, often using a variety of materials tailored to the exact explanation they are giving. *Practice* usually entails controlled-for-form exercises, where learners practice the target form by filling in the blank, answering true/false questions and other worksheet-type materials,

---

[13] In a CL sense, "the fact that abstract senses of words are related to their more literal uses is sometimes referred to by cognitive linguists as linguistic motivation" (Littlemore & Juchen-Grundmann 2010:7).

while the instructor monitors all answers and offers corrective feedback. After this stage, students do more mechanical work and complete exercises from their worksheet. Finally, in the *Production* stage, learners are encouraged to use language in a more open, communicative way, with role-playing exercises, collaborative activities, or group discussions. The idea is to simulate ways in which the target form(s) would be used outside of the classroom, in "the real world." But this poses a problem for learners because every rule that is applied to grammatical forms without taking their meaning(s) into account will lack any operational value beyond the ad hoc examples provided during in-class work (Llopis-García et al. 2012: 47. OT).

If the phrase "*presentation practice production lesson plan*" is entered on a search engine, 46.7 million results appear. In the "featured snippet" box with content that best represents that search, a site by the British Council is high-lighted as relevant, so I have included it here as a prototypical example of a "grammar as an object of study" lesson plan, especially because it mentions that the PPP model "works well as it can be used for most isolated grammatical items," which is precisely the point of contention of this section – there is no such thing as "isolated grammar" and as Toth and Davin (2016: 152) argue, it is "impossible to truly isolate grammatical forms from purposeful use through practice, as though doing so were a dress rehearsal for some more "authentic" language performance later."

1.2.3 Grammar Is Still the Apple of Discord in L2 Teaching

Grammar, pedagogical grammar, communicative grammar, descriptive grammar, inductive grammar, what kind of grammar, how to teach grammar, how much to teach, when to teach . . . – these concepts and questions continue to be a topic of contention and disagreement among instructors, curricular designers, linguists, and textbook publishers alike.

As mentioned in Section 1.2, over the last forty years, L2 instruction has been informed by fields such as SLA, cognitive science, educational technology, or the psychology of education. Methodological approaches to class dynamics, the development of communicative skills, and the teaching of sociocultural aspects, to name a few, have been explored and reimagined. However, in agreement with Tyler (2012), Kissling et al. (2018) point out that whatever the methodological improvement, the teaching of grammar "appears to assume that once [it] is introduced, the best path to learning is for students to memorize the rules and the many, seemingly arbitrary meanings associated with a single lexical unit" (p. 229).

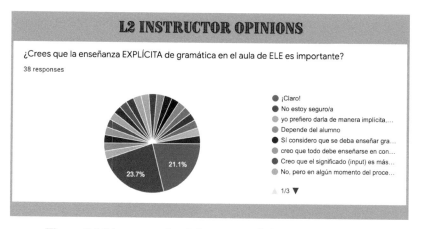

Figure 1 L2 instructors' opinions on explicit grammar teaching

To further highlight the diversity of pedagogical beliefs about grammar teaching, I will provide a practical example. Every year since 2014, I have taught an online seminar about cognitive linguistic approaches to the teaching of Spanish/L2 grammar. Since 2016 and at the beginning of the course, I ask participants (instructors of Spanish of different backgrounds and experience) whether they think that the *explicit* teaching of grammar in the classroom is important. I give them two clear-cut options (*Of course!/I'm not sure*) but allow them to type in their own answer as well. Figure 1, from the 2020 edition, shows their answers.

Red represents the option *I'm not sure*, chosen by nine instructors, and blue is *Of course!*, with eight respondents. The remaining 55.2 percent of answers (21) are as diverse as the colors in the graph, which (within the limited but interesting sample) goes to further prove the point that grammar is a "hot spot," since everyone has something to say about it, whether to agree or to disagree. In fact, in the aggregate count of 2016 to 2021 (not counting 2020 because it is provided in the figure), from a total of 103 respondents, 57.2 percent were in favor of teaching explicit grammar, 16.5 percent were not sure, and 26.2 percent had an opinion that merited a longer explanation, whether in agreement or disagreement.

1.3 Final Considerations

Teaching grammar and vocabulary in the L2 classroom, as widely discussed, is done mostly separately, at different points during the lesson plan and throughout levels of competence. While it is not wrong to dedicate separate time to either during the course of a session, what the ideas in these pages propose, however, is to teach both with a similar understanding. Cognitive linguistic approaches to language, based on human sensorimotor experience and influenced by the culture of discourse communities (and not by arbitrary restrictions), offer "numerous pedagogical alternatives ... that are much more attractive than some of the traditional proposals (for example, memorizing bilingual glossaries)" (Piquer-Píriz & Boers 2019: 59. OT).

So let us see what makes ACL a methodological option for the L2 instruction setting and how its principles and tenets have led to its increasing popularity among language instructors.

2 The Realized Potential of Applied Cognitive Linguistics and L2 Instruction

The positive aspect of ACL is that many language instructors are already bringing it into their classrooms, and oftentimes they are not even aware of it. If you are an L2 instructor, consider these few questions:

- Do you try to bring "some kind of comprehensive logic" into the formal and descriptive explanations that your textbook provides?
- Do you explain grammatical concepts and illustrate lexical items by way of gesturing, moving around the classroom, and using all objects within reach to represent meaning?
- Does your board fill up with stick figures, arrows, and shapes when explaining prepositions?
- Do you ask your students "how do you say this in your L1?" and then try to bridge the gap between their language and the L2 by finding common ground?

If "yes" was the answer to any of these questions, your teaching has strong ACL components already.

The advantage of the ACL approach is that it is highly intuitive because it is based on the experiential nature of language. If one understands that language emerges from human interaction with the world, it follows that linguistic structure represents those interactions. And it starts early on in life when we do not even have a linguistic structure to explicitly communicate with. Lee (2001: 18) observed that "one of our earliest and most basic cognitive achievements as infants is to acquire an understanding of objects and of the way in which they relate to each other in physical space." Babies spend hours looking at the mobiles hanging above their cradles and decoding color, distance, motion, or sound. Their communication is restricted to physical and sensory traits: warmth from being physically held, coldness when that proximity disappears, nearness as a sign for interaction, and distance for the lack thereof. As infants

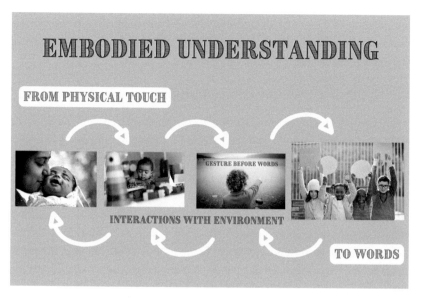

Figure 2 Embodied understanding

grow, the next stage in communication is gesture-based: children point to what they want or need, toward their family members, or to signal recognition of elements in their surroundings (by the time they are able to say *doggie*!, the pointing gesture has long been in use). So, if humans are already communicating long before linguistic statements are used, does it not follow that those statements will directly build from *that* communication? Figure 2 portrays how we evolve from communicating with physical touch alone to using gestures, to speaking words, and how the natural progression is related.

From a CL perspective, language is experiential – it arises from physical interaction with the world and it permeates the whole linguistic system and its grammatical structure. This physical interaction gives way to embodied aspects in language that become conventionalized in discourse communities through their systematic usage. Consider the following examples:

- They have a very *close* relationship
- I don't know why you're so *distant* with me
- Her mother was *bursting* with pride
- Things progressed at a *glacial* pace.

The italicized words (*close, distant, bursting, glacial*) are all based on sensori-motor observations: spatial perceptions for the first two, the body as a container for the third, and for the last one, the physical observation of the speed of motion of glaciers in nature. The use of these representational features is figurative and not literal, but the fact that we understand their underlying, original meaning is what is known as *motivation* in CL, and it is what puts *embodiment* at the core of every linguistic system.

2.1 Space, Embodiment, and Sensorimotor Experience

In the teaching and learning of L2s, what would happen if motion, physics, the analysis of spatial features, and the perceptual experiences of our five senses were present in the grammatical constructions of the languages we know and/ or wish to learn? The visual examples from Figure 2 illustrate the relationship between embodied understanding and embodied language (*from physical touch to words*), and this relationship extends to all linguistic categories, from nouns to verbs to prepositions to articles, and everything in between. Embodied aspects in language facilitate communication, provide access to semantic and morphological cues in the L2, and help bridge the gap between languages. From this perspective, form-meaning connections do not have to be or have to seem arbitrary, for they are often rooted in human experience, which departs from the "foreign language" construct and creates meaningful awareness for learners. Linguistic motivation plays a role here too because it "stimulates the cognitive abilities of students and increases their attention to a series of linguistic phenomena" (Piquer-Píriz & Boers 2019: 54).

The previous paragraph can be illustrated with an example from Spanish: the periphrastic construction to speak about the future [*ir*+*a*+infinitive], which is equivalent to the *going-to future* in English. In both languages, this construction is used to refer to a future event, but it is different from the simple future in Spanish and the [*will*+verb] construction in English. So why would there be an additional option to talk about the future? Embodiment, space, and motion provide insight into the grammatical structure (Figure 3).

The verb *ir/go* has a core meaning of motion: *we go somewhere,* meaning that we move from one place to another, usually with a specific destination in mind. The preposition *a/to*, which at its core meaning or *prototype* (Section 2.4) refers to a "forward motion towards a destination," provides semantic direction and points to the final location of the motion. Both components are based on the sensorimotor understanding of all humans, as *motion* and *destination* are two sides of the same experience – someone departs from a location in order to reach a different destination: *voy a mi casa* (*I go home*) or *vamos al supermercado* (*we go to the grocery store*) are both examples of this idea, where "home" or "the grocery store" are destinations to which the speakers arrived from somewhere else.

Now, because sensorimotor experience is universal, common to everyone, and already exists in language, it can serve as a point of access for more complex and

Figure 3 The embodiment of the periphrastic future

abstract communicative needs. Thus, we can transfer *what we know* about "motion" and "destination" to concepts like "intention" and "goal" and use the overlap of their common ground to create new meanings. This transfer of knowledge from the physical domains to more abstract, conceptual areas is known as *metaphor* (Section 2.3) and it bridges the gap between knowledge we all share and new events, feelings, emotions, or backgrounds that we want to communicate.

In the example of the periphrastic future, also known as "future of intention" in L2 settings, the motion of the verb *ir* is conceptualized as *intention* (wanting to make a change from one state to another); the preposition, with its "forward motion towards a destination" reinforces the *intent* of the verb and provides a (figurative) straight path to the final destination, which becomes the *end goal* of the intention. The final piece of the construction is the infinitive, the impersonal form of a verb: there is no conjugation or information on who, what, when, or how the action is performed, so it simply conveys the *idea* of an action, that is, the *end goal* itself.

Figure 3 provides a visual example of this figurative transfer: *Voy a sacar muy buenas notas* (*I am going to get very good grades*), where *voy* is the conjugated form in the first person in the present tense. The literal motion of the verb becomes fictive through the intention of studying consistently (*point of departure*) in order to create the change to the good grades at the end of the year (*end goal*). The relationship between the intention and the good grades is reinforced by the preposition *a*, which outlines the *path of transition* (i.e. going to the library every day, attending class on a regular basis . . .) with the *end goal* of the great report card in sight. And finally, *sacar buenas notas/getting good grades*, with the infinitive *sacar* (to *get* or *achieve*) is the actual *end goal/objective* of the fictive motion of the verb.

Making these connections in the L2 classroom allows for a more connected and intuitive access to grammatical constructions, especially also in the nomenclature used with the students, whereby we may introduce *the future of intention*, a more relatable concept than the more "technical" label of *periphrastic future*. Teaching materials that incorporate sensorimotor and spatial awareness for grammatical form are not only possible but desirable for a more meaningful and "less foreign" learning experience. Figure 4a and 4b[14] show B1-level teaching materials used in an online course in 2021 to explain and practice this construction.

The first slide includes two animated stickers (a running figure carrying an arrow and a boy riding a moving plane) that help conceptualize the literal motion of the verb *ir/to go* and make a visual transition to the fictive motion of personal intention. The second slide, aimed at meaningful practice and thematic to the COVID-19 pandemic, provides a relatable example to motivate students to create their own output by using provided temporal references to help further emphasize the future-dependent context versus that of the moment of enunciation.

(a)　　　　　　　　　　　　　　　(b)

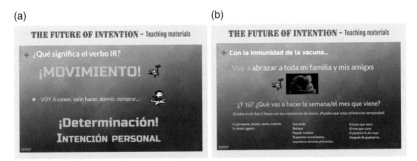

Figure 4 (a) Teaching embodied grammar: theory,
and **(b)** teaching embodied grammar: practice

---

[14]　Slide 1: *What does the verb TO GO mean? Motion! I am going to eat, go out, do, sleep, buy . . . Determination! Personal Intention.*

　　Slide 2: *With the immunity of the vaccination . . . I am going to hug my whole family and friends.*

　　What about you? What are you going to do next week/month? Write two sentences on the chat with your intentions for the future. You can use these temporal references! [Examples of situated temporal markers/constructions.]

These examples show that activating the experiential knowledge and sensori-motor awareness of learners in order to motivate grammatical structures provides a more interesting insight into the linguistic system than the mere presentation of a rule devoid of semantic value. "In essence, promoting insight means reducing the perceived arbitrariness of the foreign language system" (Taylor 2008: 57).

2.2 Conceptualization and Construal

Because embodied aspects are a universal experience of humans, studying other languages through this perspective facilitates communication and builds bridges between what students know from their L1 and what they are learning in the L2. We can make other languages more accessible by focusing on the common *conceptualization* rather than on the different *construals* they offer. Let us illustrate the difference between these terms through the visual representation of an English-Spanish lexical unit: *to make a decision* versus *tomar una decisión* (literally, *to take a decision*) (Figure 5).

Conceptualization refers to the understanding of the world that language users have, while *construal* focuses on how that understanding is linguistically expressed. In the example from English, *to make a decision* accentuates the creative thought process that must happen for someone to resolve something. Spanish, on the other hand, focuses on the conceptual realm of *choice*: what options are available during the thought process, and which will be the final pick. It is worth noticing how both expressions seem to be part of the same general mental scene on how we understand the decision-making process (*conceptualization*), but they focus on different segments of that process for the actual expression of the idea (*construal*). However, as Suárez-Campos et al. (2020: 83) point out, students' by-default "lack of awareness of conceptual similarities between languages seems to a problematic area that hinders

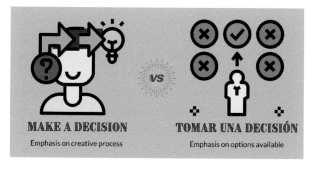

Figure 5 Conceptualization and construal

the correct comprehension of metaphorical expressions." Because of this issue, teaching either expression in Spanish or English through the explicit *motivation* of these segments can: (a) contribute to a more accessible understanding of the expression; (b) foster a better chance at remembering the collocation because of this meaningful understanding, and (c) build the learner's *metaphorical competence*. As MacArthur (2017: 415) points out: "If a learner engages deeply with target language forms and meanings – that is, makes some kind of mental effort – this is likely to result in the information being committed to long term memory." This mental effort, then, needs to be explicitly trained through an instruction that makes learners aware of these similarities.

2.3 Metaphor and Metaphorical Competence

When considering the concept of *metaphor*, one may think back to high school literature classes, the analysis of poetry, and the rhetorical devices used by the great masters. Metaphor, in this context, was what turned white teeth into pearls, what brought on the bright red color of blood to describe lips, or what compared budding flowers to youth. In this context, metaphors were stylistic elements that could elevate one's writing and added creativity to communication skills. We learned, in short, that it was an optional tool to be used for a communicative "wow effect," but not that metaphor *is* "an inevitable part of everyday human communication, let alone everyday human thought and reasoning" (Kövecses 2010:10).

The publication of *Metaphors We Live By* (Lakoff & Johnson 1980) highlighted their status as a cognitive operation of the first order, necessary for humans to translate the language of the mind into the more accessible, easier-to-understand words we use to communicate and understand one another. In general, metaphors explain complex concepts via accessible images that can be easily processed and comprehended because they are based on shared experiences and collective memory traits. *Life*, for instance, even though it is a shared human experience, is also a highly individual one. And in order to communicate around individual differences, we pick another, more relatable concept that is rooted in our real-world experience. Therefore, to talk about *life* from a place of shared knowledge, the concept of a *journey* becomes available. We think of *life* in terms of a *journey* because we can find many instances in which both seem to overlap and make sense from an experiential point of view. In CL, the instances of *life* and *journey* are called *domains*, and they are mental categories that help organize our knowledge and access information when we need to communicate. Metaphors establish that one domain can be understood in terms of another, and in the relationship between LIFE and JOURNEY (called

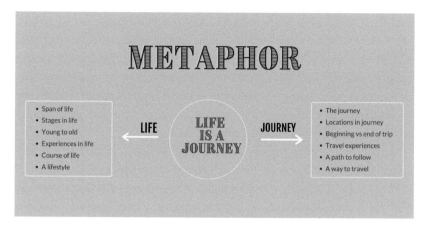

Figure 6 Conceptual metaphor and mappings

a *conceptual metaphor*), the span of an entire life is seen as a journey. Going from *young* to *old* in life is understood as the *beginning* and the *end* of a journey. Also, what is experienced through life may resemble moments during a trip, or a lifestyle may resemble a way to travel. Figure 6 offers a few more connections, also known as *mappings*.

Metaphors, then, connect the conceptual system in our mind with the "real language" we use in everyday communication, and they are "intrinsic to language because metaphor is intrinsic to thought" (Nacey 2017: 503).

The following examples are real-life *linguistic metaphors* of the conceptual metaphor LIFE IS A JOURNEY:

(1) Every person has a *path* in life, one that is intertwined with the fate of the earth (Café con Libros, @cafeconlibros_bk, 12/19/2021 on Instagram).
(2) How to *navigate* racist conversations this holiday (Naomi and Natalia, @everydayracism_, 12/1/2020 on Instagram).
(3) We've *come a long way*, but there is still a long, *long way to go* (The Corpus of Contemporary American English[15]).
(4) Ladies and gentlemen, may we present the design economy. It is the *crossroads* where prosperity and technology meet culture and marketing (TIME Magazine Corpus[16]).

It can be easily noted that all instances are commonplace samples of language we use in general conversation, and while (1) may be considered more poetic, it is still fairly frequent. Also, consider how all four examples are not about literal

---

[15] www.english-corpora.org/coca/.
[16] www.english-corpora.org/time/.

travel. They refer to life events and express them with language that is reminiscent of the experience of travel, thus finding an accessible common ground for those involved in the interaction. Earlier, at the beginning of Section 2, we saw examples such as "They have a very *close* relationship" or "I don't know why you're so *distant* with me," where EMOTIONS (the abstract *target domain*) are conceptualized in terms of DISTANCE (a much more concrete, easy-to-grasp concept, also known as the *source domain*).

Language is full of metaphors because they organize our abstract comprehension of the world around us and explain complex constructs (such as emotions, ideas, theories, or relationships) with concepts that come from our collective experience as human beings, or as part of a given discourse community. Metaphors convert our inner language into social communicative events. As speakers are influenced by their sensorimotor experience, as well as by the common experiences of their society, they will assign this experiential meaning to linguistic forms, thus facilitating common ground for mutual understanding. This is called *metaphorical competence* (MC),[17] and it is the ability to both understand and produce metaphors.

Metaphorical competence is an integrative part of our general *communicative competence*, which also addresses grammatical, sociolinguistic, discursive, or pragmatic competences (Cenoz Iragui 2004). It activates and motivates figurative language, thus contributing to a more accessible understanding of language, since it highlights the relationship between abstract and experiential domains and makes their relationship explicit to L2 learners (Ibarretxe-Antuñano, Cadierno, & Castañeda Castro 2019). "Figurative language is not an ornamental linguistic manifestation, but the natural product of mental mechanisms that allow us to understand abstract concepts by establishing analogical (metaphorical) or associational (metonymic) relationships with more concrete concepts based on our physical, social, and cultural experiences" (Piquer-Píriz & Boers 2019: 58. OT). For the L1, this ability is largely an unconscious process, but its development in the L2 classroom by means of explicit instruction has enormous – albeit complex – pedagogical potential, because "guessing the meaning of a figurative sense through a core sense provides the second language learner with an opportunity for a precise elaboration, enabling [them] to incorporate the figurative sense into a semantic network more effectively and recall it later" (Verspoor & Lowie 2003: 569).

---

[17] In the field of first language acquisition it is known as *metaphoric competence* and it differs in the naming from *metaphorical competence* in order to differentiate both as different processes (Danesi 1992), since the former is acquired and the second must be learned. I have found both labels in the field of CL and L2. *Metaphorical competence* will be used throughout this text.

In the L1, MC is encoded in a person's *encyclopedic knowledge* (their general knowledge of the world), while L2 pedagogical treaties such as the CERF include its basis under the *general competences* that any L2 teaching methodology should address. These competences relate to *declarative knowledge* (sociocultural understanding, intercultural awareness, and knowledge of the world) or to *the ability to learn*, which entails "knowing how, or being disposed, to discover 'otherness' – whether the other is another language, another culture, other people, or new areas of knowledge" (CERF: 12). For the case of MC, even though it is not explicitly included in the current models of communicative competence (Canale & Swain 1980 or Bachman 1990[18]), it belongs within, just the same as other sub-competences that have been added over time: sociocultural (Kramsch 1998), digital (Juan-Lázaro & Biel 2020), or interactional (Young 2011).

2.3.1 Issues of Metaphorical Competence in L2

MC shows the conceptualization of the linguistic world of a discourse community and as MacArthur (2017: 413) points out, "since it is such an important part of everyday language use, one would expect that attention to metaphor would be an integral part of every language course designed for learners of a second or foreign language (S/FL). However, the simple truth is that it seldom, if ever, is." This is true for MC, but mostly also for CL in general (Achard 2008, 2018; De Knop, Boers, & De Rycker 2010; Tyler 2012; Tyler, Huang, & Jan 2018; Llopis-García & Hijazo-Gascón 2019; Piquer-Píriz & Alejo-González 2020). The problem stems from an unfortunate "catch-22" situation: it is hard to conduct research with MC because learners decode the L2 in a very literal way, and because L2 instruction hardly incorporates MC-based pedagogy from the elementary levels (or at all), it is very difficult to make learners aware of motivated language, embodiment, semantic networks, and even metaphor itself.

In CL, the consensus seems to be that the activation of metaphorical competence is very hard to achieve without proper, direct, systematic, and explicit instruction (Acquaroni Muñoz 2008; Littlemore 2009, 2010; Azuma & Littlemore 2010; Masid Blanco 2017. Also, see Nacey 2017 for an overview of studies on L2 and metaphor comprehension). This is because, as mentioned earlier, "language learners deal with metaphor in a much more mechanical, analytic way than native speakers. Teaching activities that are designed to help learners deal with creative metaphor should take account of this fact" (Littlemore 2009: 102. Also MacArthur & Littlemore 2008). Low (2020) reports on recent

---

[18] Although see Littlemore & Low 2006 for an inclusion of MC within the Bachman model.

studies that have been conducted with German and Chinese learners of English (Niemeier 2017 and Pan 2019, respectively) and, like many others who deal with empirical research, remarks on the unlikely generalizability of the studies, given both methodology issues and participant pool size. And while these concerns are valid and there is an urgent need to empirically validate cognitive linguistic approaches in L2, the reality of the classroom experience requires different scopes and focus.

The L2 classroom is not an orderly and controlled experiment, but rather, a vibrant, ever-changing, and dynamic experience where competences are often intertwined when vocabulary or grammar are at the center of the lesson. The restrictive settings that are put in place during empirical studies (strict attendance, highly curbed student proficiency levels, no homework/ practice outside class between tests, etc.) do not resemble the daily experience of the language classroom, where learners will learn new words or practice grammatical constructions through instruction, and also while reading a text, building a conversation, or working on a creative and multimodal assignment.

There is yet another obstacle MC encounters in its path to become a staple in L2 teaching methodologies: the generalized belief in the teaching community that metaphor and the understanding of figurative language are more suited to and should be reserved for advanced levels. In fact, the Curricular Plan of the Cervantes Institute (2006), which adapts the CERF to Spanish/ L2, includes metaphorical expressions for the first time at the B2 level, which is equivalent to a high-intermediate or advanced proficiency level. This happens because of the ornamental function for which metaphor is widely known, and because "metaphors are still felt by some to be largely literary and thus recondite, obscure, and difficult. According to this view, metaphor reflects an advanced use by a minority of speakers and there is little justification for exposing most learners to it" (Littlemore & Low 2006: 269).

Such a view is unfounded, though, especially when considering that this competence "is a basic feature of native-speaker competence" (Danesi 1993: 493) and that native speakers "process conventional expressions in a rapid, automatized way, at times without much active thought about basic meanings and concepts" (Littlemore & Low 2006: 272). Language learners, however, are in a very different situation, since they are unaware of the literal versus figurative senses a word/construction may have. Without explicit instruction and training on metaphorical thinking, it is very unlikely that learners will actively engage in figurative language understanding and/or transfer among the languages they speak. And yet, MC can add an enormous advantage for linguistic processing when dealing with the L2. In the words of Acquaroni Muñoz and Suárez-Campos (2019: 374. OT), "MC is a skill that requires the activation of the same strategies and cognitive processes in both languages, such as episodic memory, analogical reasoning, the interpretation of context or associative fluency." Also, as Suárez-Campos (2020) found in a study with Bulgarian learners of Spanish at the A2, B1, and B2 CERF levels, "the greater or lesser use of metaphorical language [by the learners at the studied levels] did not depend so much on their [general] proficiency in L2, but on whether they had trained their metaphorical competence [in the L2]" (p. 406. OT).

From these ideas, it follows that introducing MC from the elementary levels would be an advisable pedagogical choice, since it would help students transfer skills *they already have* in their L1 to the learning of vocabulary and grammar in L2, and thus develop a *metaphorical awareness* to improve their ability to: (a) reason and infer meaning; (b) memorize and better access L2 content; and (c) build a motivated learning of the target language. There is empirical research showing that "informing second language learners of the motivation behind the figurative meaning of idioms can be helpful in the sense that this helps to make that meaning more memorable" (MacArthur 2017: 417. Also Littlemore & Low 2006 and Boers & Lindstromberg 2008).

To conclude this section, considering that learning an L2 "largely means recategorizing many aspects of the world," using ACL and MC to teach "adds a focus on a theory of grammar that points to cognitive processing and language use as its foundation" (Tyler & Huang 2018: 5–6). Systematically addressing embodiment, conceptualization, perspective, the motivation behind idiomatic expressions, and normalizing the ubiquity of figurative language in the L2 classroom gives structure and organization to the apparent randomness of the target language, both in grammar and in vocabulary. Nacey (2017: 510) makes a strong point in saying that "the integration of activities focusing on various aspects of metaphoric competence into standard teaching aids and tools (such as textbooks) is crucial if research ... is to have much real impact on language teaching, learning, and assessment." Methodologically, this can be done via ACL tweaks on classic classroom staples such as visual input, gestures, physical enactments, or more recent takes such as mapped-out texts, mind maps, attention to collocations, etc. (see Sections 3 and 4 for a more detailed account of pedagogical tools for the ACL classroom).

2.3.2 What Metaphorical Competence Can Look Like in the L2 Classroom

Let us consider two examples from an ACL-based Spanish elementary course (A1 on the CERF) for vocabulary learning, which could also easily be used in the English counterpart with Spanish learners. The first example centers on the semantic network that the polysemous verb *llevar* (*to wear/carry/take*) can build (see Figure 7 below).

During the A1 level, students will come across the more embodied, representational uses of the verb *llevar*: carrying something and wearing something. These two meanings will be learned separately and will appear explicitly in different chapters of the textbook. The third meaning, which is figurative, belongs in intermediate to advanced levels (mostly for peninsular Spanish use) and will be learned, if at all, well after the other two. *Llevar* has other meanings, of course, many of which are also figurative, but if the point is to train students' MC from the beginning of their language learning experience, this figurative use (extended from the embodied idea of *point of contact* that the other two convey) can work well. All three uses are represented on a gradual scale, with *wearing* a clothing item conceptualized as a full-body experience (because it will profile a specific part of your body that *completes* your whole outfit). The second level will be to *carry* something, like a cup of tea, a book, a backpack … something that does not remain with you at all times and that affects your physical domain only partially. For the third and figurative level, the focus is on events that are important and impact you emotionally over time, so you "carry them with you": the relationship you are in, the amount of time since giving up smoking, the progress made with exercising, etc. This figurative

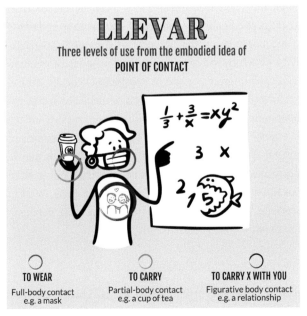

Figure 7 Metaphorical competence: A1-level example

use activates the conceptual metaphor of EVENTS ARE OBJECTS and conceptualizes a romantic relationship as "something invisible" you carry with you as you move through your day, much like a backpack or a sweater.

Presenting all three meanings together when introducing the verb (even when not all three belong in the same proficiency level) contributes to:

- Training students to see embodiment first, and then identifying semantic extensions via metaphor
- Normalizing analogical reasoning between domains in the L2 via understanding of the images in their L1. At the same time, this can activate awareness of conceptual similarities between their L1 and L2 and foster interlinguistic understanding
- Making figurative meanings salient and motivated in the target language, starting at the A1 level and training students to "see language" as they move across competence levels
- Making learners used to the fact that language is symbolic and that meanings can be interdependent, even if the usage events are not. Work with mind maps or collocations (Section 3.2) also helps in this way
- Developing agency so students may know when to use either meaning according to their communicative intent.

The second material motivates the semantics behind the morphology and phonology of adjectives in both languages (see Figure 8).

For the case of English, the word *dizzy* has a buzzing sound that phonetically embodies the ringing in one's ears when nausea, headache, or physical discomfort ail a person. The field of cognitive phonology supports this approach to motivated sound, since it considers that "the brain is [also] part of the physical

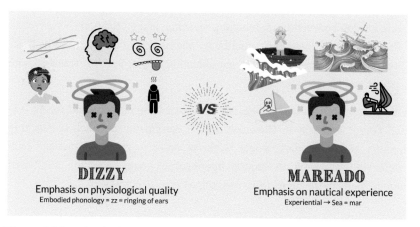

Figure 8 Metaphorical competence: phonological and morphological mappings

world and from the perceptual level, it encodes the sounds it receives through the ear. This implies that there is nothing in the continuum from the physical to the cognitive that separates phonetics (physical) from phonology (cognitive)" (Mompeán & Mompeán 2012: 320. OT). The (phonetic) motivation of the word places the conceptualization on the physiological quality derived from the experience, and it is a familiar experience for many. The suffix -y adds the adjectival nuance that many other adjectives also have (*sunny, creamy,* or *fluffy,* to name a few). Piquer-Píriz and Boers (2019) also posit that making students aware of sound patterns that can be associated to linguistic forms in the L2 can contribute to their retention and memorability (p. 60).

In the case of Spanish, the underlying event might not ever be endured by many, but the motivation of the nautical experience (*mareado* comes from the Latin *mare, maris*: i.e. "the alteration of spatial understanding, with the sensation of instability accompanied, sometimes, by lightheadedness, vertigo, nausea, and even loss of consciousness"[19] from being rocked by the sea) certainly lives in the collective and historical memory of the Spanish-speaking community. The suffix -*eado* in adjectives, additionally, adds a nuance of "thoroughness" to the quality, because it also forms the past participle of the -ar verb conjugation and therefore brings aspectual completion to the action (as in *salteado = thoroughly sautéed, moqueado = thoroughly snotted, canjeado = fully exchanged, estropeado = thoroughly spoiled*, etc.). For *mareado*, the word *mar* (*sea*) and -*eado* as "suffix of thoroughness" form a concept that when explained to students:

- Activates encyclopedic knowledge and makes the learning of lexis more meaningful and connected, thus creating a more memorable learning experience
- Makes the symbolic nature of language very explicit by highlighting the relationship between form, function, meaning, and motivation
- Profiles the morphological structure by adding semanticity beyond its functional use, making the learning and retention of grammatical features more salient and likely.

Both examples of teaching materials presented here were created for an A1-level course and aim to showcase how a systematic approach to teaching grammar and vocabulary would work, in order to "provide students with a coherent framework to acquire figurative language, avoiding traditional learning by memorization" (Suárez-Campos et al 2020: 91).

---

[19] OT from Segura Munguía, S. (2014) *Diccionario etimológico de Medicina*. Universidad de Deusto.

At this point, several pedagogical aspects about MC that are relevant for ACL teaching come together:

Meaningful learning – In order to forge an accessible path to motivated learning, activating MC in the classroom gives students insights on how the target language works. This can foster a pedagogy that does not give learners the impression that the multiple meanings of a preposition are random and must be learned as a list or individually, on an "as-they-show-up" basis: "being able to explain the meaningful systematicity of a word's polysemy network potentially lessens the learner's memory load and helps provide strategies for figuring out the meaning of new uses they encounter in native speaker discourse" (Tyler & Huang 2018: 6). In the words of Langacker (2008a: 72): "With proper instruction, the learning of a usage is thus a matter of grasping the semantics "spin" it imposes, a far more natural and enjoyable process than sheer memorization".

Figure 9, on the A1-level teaching of demonstrative adjectives in Spanish (*this/these, that/those* in English), uses space and embodied cognition to show the *three levels of literal and figurative distance* expressed by these forms and that convey the perspective of the speaker on objects and ideas. By using the concepts of *here/aquí-acá, there/ahí,* and *over there/allí-allá*, learners can equate the identifiable, distance-based information with linguistic forms and not only speak of the literal proximity of objects (i.e., *this cat*), but also of figurative distance, as in *those were the days*.

L1-L2 affinity – The encyclopedic knowledge and personal experiences of the students are integrated in the L2 so that affective bonds can naturally occur. This can bring about a *"deforeignizing"*[20] of the target language, where

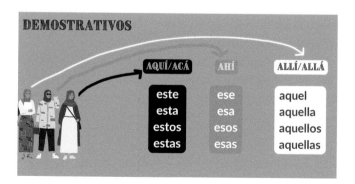

Figure 9 Space-based grammar

---

[20] "To deforeignize" is not an actual verb, but its coinage seems relevant, given the pervasiveness of teaching methodologies that present lists of vocabulary to go with a lesson plan or a textbook

conceptual similarities that yield differences in construal are normalized, and students can feel more familiarity with the L2 from the known territory of their L1 (and other languages they may speak). The advantage of normalizing *interlinguistic* reasoning to foster *intralinguistic* understanding and community building in the classroom is also in line with the advocacy for translanguaging in the language classroom. This is because the inclusion of all languages known to students and instructors as a stepping stone from which to construe the L2 enables "processes through which both multilingual and monolingual individuals use multimodal resources to construct meanings, shape experiences and perform identities in their social encounters in specific, superdiverse contexts" (Conteh 2018: 473).

Learning systematicity – Working with learners from a place of systematic motivation of figurative language and metaphorical awareness will create coherence and establish a pattern to learn grammar and vocabulary. Boers (2013), for instance, discusses the learning of emotions and the pedagogical advantages of using conceptual metaphors. Instructors can incorporate the ANGER IS HEAT conceptual metaphor to contextualize examples such as the following, extracted from the CoCA: (a) I'm really sorry I *blew up at* you; (b) Ukraine continued to *simmer with* unrest Tuesday; and (c) This person has created negativity and hostility in our family for years now. I do not need to *add fuel to the fire*. He points out that "it seems natural to talk about emotions such as anger in terms of heat, because of the physiological changes that coincide with passionate emotions" (p. 213). In this scenario, Boers proposes that instructors and students can engage in brainstorming why the linguistic instances make sense from the domain interaction of the conceptual metaphor. Also, they can provide examples of how their L1 or other languages they know conceptualize the domain of ANGER. "Learners can be asked to group figurative expressions under the headings of conceptual metaphors or to identify their common source domains themselves" (p. 213), which would strengthen their MC by training their semantic elaboration skills and confirm a perception of systematicity for what would have been unrelated instances in their vocabulary list otherwise.

---

unit, and that provide charts of grammar to be practiced in context throughout. This manner of teaching perpetuates the "otherness" of the target language, dims the representational nature of language, and brands the language as an object of study. From an L2 instruction perspective, language is not a phenomenon to observe and document and it should not be learned in isolation from usage and its social and cultural implications. An ACL-based approach aims at dispensing with the perceived "foreignness" of the L2, seeking access to the conceptualizations of the linguistic system, the motivation of meaning, and the cultural representations that every *living* language affords.

2.4 Categorization and Prototypes

In everyday L1 experience, when dealing with the tremendous amount of information that we process at any given moment, human cognition relies on the process of *categorization*. This process helps us "organize our knowledge of the world not into discrete, neat categories, but into messy, overlapping categories ..., [with] some members of a category that are more central than others" (Taylor & Littlemore, 2014: 6). These central members are called *prototypes*, and they are the most archetypal members of the mental image they represent. For instance, if we consider the category of BIRDS, a robin would be more prototypical than an emu (see Figure 10). A prototype, then, includes most of the qualities from the category, and from it we can move through other members to help us see that even though the emu does not fly, it still has wings, a beak, feathers, two legs, and lays eggs, all BIRD-like traits.

The interesting thing about categories is that they not only help us organize information from the world around, but they also apply to language as a system and are central to how we understand and systematize the linguistic information we learn, know, and use. Starting at the core with the prototype, we build semantic extensions, also called *radial networks*, which make possible the transposition of criteria for those more peripheral meanings. These meanings, from a linguistic perspective, will include figurative and metaphorical uses, while the prototype will be based on a spatial and/or representational meaning. The degree of membership of the peripheral members will be determined by their association with the prototype, as represented in the form of a spider's web in Figure 11.

For the teaching and learning of L2s, working with prototypes and their radial networks offers systemic and motivated explanations of grammatical items that

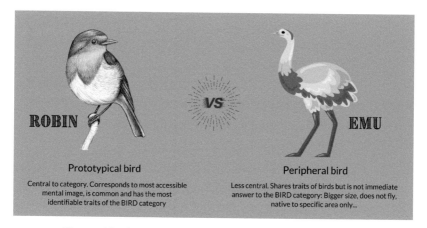

Figure 10 The BIRD prototype versus a peripheral member

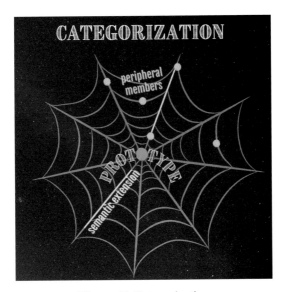

Figure 11 Categorization

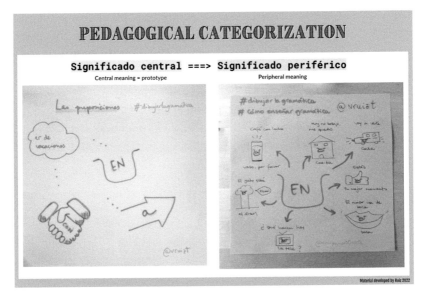

Figure 12 Pedagogical uses of categorization for Spanish prepositions

are otherwise perceived as random and unconnected. Figure 12 shows a classroom-based example of Spanish/L2, where prepositional prototypes (*significado central/core meaning*) and semantic extensions (*significado periférico/ peripheral meaning*) are used (Ruiz 2022).

If prototypes are based on physical-spatial relationships, then all members of a linguistic category will extend their meaning from there and create a related network of associations that will help learners understand different uses of the same word. And because physical and spatial relationships stem from salient human experience, they become more accessible. In the language classroom, their learning is thus more user-friendly and less arbitrary.

2.4.1 The Case of Prepositions: Categorization and Prototypes in Action

Figure 12 offered an example of how the organization of linguistic information via categorization and prototypes brings a pedagogical application to L2 prepositions. These are highly frequent and polysemous words, and these two defining features make them, as any L2 instructor will confirm, very difficult to teach and very confusing to learn (Lam 2009; Tyler et al 2011; Mendo Murillo 2014; Llopis-García 2015, 2019b). This is mostly because preposition uses are learned individually as they relate to the different notional-functional directives that textbooks introduce chapter by chapter, such as *giving directions, asking for information, using spatial references, expressing intentions*, etc.

Prepositions are present from the very first pages of every L2 textbook, but a quick look at a few of them will confirm that they are rarely taught explicitly at the introductory levels (Llopis-García 2015, 2019b). This results in students being exposed to a corpus of arbitrary meanings, ad hoc examples to the communicative functions they are in, or in collocations and periphrastic uses, which further obscures their stand-alone semantic value.

CL, however, offers an approach aimed at facilitating "the retention of prepositional uses and better [equipping] learners to deal with novel or unfamiliar contexts" (Lam 2009: 4). For English, Tyler and Evans's (2003) work, *The Semantics of English Prepositions: Spatial Scenes, Embodied Meaning, and Cognition*, is a key study. The starting point of their proposal was related to the prototypical meaning underlying all prepositions: "If the embodiment of experience indeed gives rise to meaning, which is to say, conceptual structure, then the concepts expressed by language should largely derive from our perception of spatial-physical experience" (p. 24). Tyler et al (2011) proposed a quick definition: "Prepositions describe a conceptualized spatial relationship between a focus element (F) and a locating or ground element (G)" (p. 184). From this notion, it is easier to see how imbuing prepositions with their visual and experiential meaning can facilitate understanding and usage by L2 learners. After all, "it is easier to apprehend the semantics of a lexical unit than that of a morphosyntactic unit" (Llopis-García et al 2012: 89. OT), and prepositions, traditionally, have been considered "function words" with less semantic and more morphosyntactic value, always

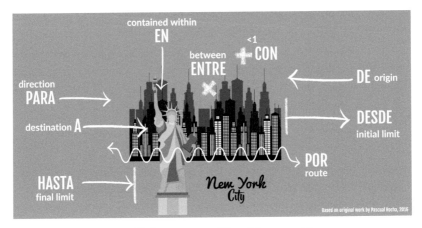

Figure 13 Prototypes of Spanish prepositions

taught in a notional context (directions, object placement, etc.) rather than by themselves. Let us see some examples from Spanish in Figure 13.

With the backdrop of New York City (the *ground* (G) that serves as location), Figure 13 shows some of the most frequent prepositions in Spanish and their spatial prototype (based on work by Pascual Rocha 2016). The first pedagogical observation is that seeing prepositions as prototypes turns the student's focus toward the core meanings. The use of graphic, visual, and Gestalt-like representations of prototypes can assist learners in recognizing and understanding patterns of use that stem from space and movement, and also from fundamental experiences common to all humans and present in all languages. From this initial approach, L2 instructors can address usage that relates to the prototype (such as spatial awareness and placement of objects in L2), and then begin "spinning the web" (see Figure 11) in order to introduce the radial network of related meanings and figurative instances.

For example, with a preposition like *hasta* (*as far as/up to a final limit*), a radial network of three uses,[21] depicted in Figure 14, can be taught.

(1) *Ella camina **hasta** el final del muelle* (*She walks **as far as** the end of the dock*) – This is the prototypical use, where there is motion up to a final line that does not get crossed. In this case, it is a literal line, since it is the end of the dock, and she would fall into the water if she went past that point.

---

[21] A common argument in the literature is that teaching the entire semantic network of a preposition would be pedagogically counterproductive and I agree. In order to teach MC and spatial awareness in the L2, and unless the teaching of multiple uses is part of a teaching objective, the pedagogical recommendation is to exemplify usage "little by little." Otherwise, we run the risk of overwhelming learners and sowing unnecessary confusion.

Figure 14 The radial network of the preposition *Hasta*

(2) *Ella trabaja **hasta** las tres* (*She works **until** three*) – This is already a figurative use. The conceptual metaphor of TIME IS SPACE is activated, and the previous physical limit becomes a final moment in time. In the example, that limit is three o'clock, the end of her workday, and at that time she leaves the office.

(3) *Ella está **hasta** aquí arriba* (*She's had it **up to** here*) – Extending a bit further away from the prototype, a figurative use in an idiomatic expression can be introduced: the final line that will not be crossed is now the end of someone's patience and goodwill.[22]

The first two uses belong (separately and unconnected from each other) in the A1 level (*spatial relationships* and *telling the time*), while the third example, being idiomatic, might appear at the B1 level when a more developed expression of emotions is learned. However, students at the elementary level are perfectly able to understand the semantic extension that draws from the prototype because the images represent conceptual scenes from reality. Chances are, too, that the languages they speak also include embodied metaphors for the expression of emotions. Materials like these provide the opportunity to engage in interlinguistic reflection and in the "de-foreignizing" of prepositions in L2, because they "provide learners with easy access to the conceptual motivation of grammar and, thus, support the creation of links between different constructions traditionally taught and learned as unrelated items" (Suñer & Roche 2019: 9)

---

[22] Note how, for the idiomatic expression, the English counterpart is also included in the visual depiction. This trains learners' MC and capitalizes on interlinguistic awareness for memorable learning.

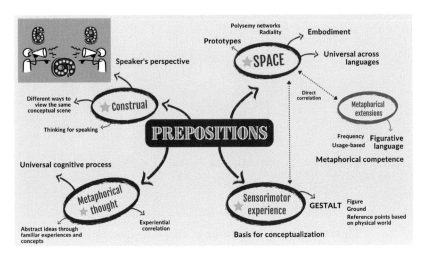

Figure 15 Prepositions: a CL overview

Working with grammatical prototypes, then, implies being able to go from a spatial core to more peripheral meanings (which can be ranked by difficulty and are usually the more figurative and idiomatic uses). Grammar "rules" take on a more relational, relatable, and connected sense – and they can be revisited as the proficiency level of students advances. Incorporating radial networks, additionally, gives order to the chaos and arbitrariness perceived by learners and affords better chances of finding logic in grammatical structures.

Prepositions, as a matter of fact, can function as the standard-bearer for ACL-based work in L2, because basically all tenets and foundational ideas of CL can be applied to the teaching and understanding of both their linguistic form and polysemic semantic values. Figure 15 showcases all the CL concepts that apply to prepositions, some of which will be discussed in the coming sections.

2.5 Perspective

Because language is, above all, a means of communication, speakers will make use of the entire linguistic system at their disposal to convey their views and communicative intent. In fact, there is nothing objective about communication, even when we attempt to describe what unfolds before our very eyes, because our minds will always filter what we observe through the lens of our own experience. As the two eye doctors featured in the photoblog *Humans of New York* (2014)[23] put it: "The eye doesn't see. The brain sees. The eye just

---

[23] Humans of New York (2014) [Facebook] June 14. www.facebook.com/humansofnewyork/posts/682848781789225:0 (Accessed 13 January 2022).

transmits. So what we see isn't only determined by what comes through the eyes. What we see is affected by our memories, our feelings, and by what we've seen before." The richness of sensory input around us can be overwhelming, but through our encyclopedic knowledge, we are able to choose the words that highlight what matters to us every time. According to Tyler & Evans (2004: 276), "a conceptual scene can be viewed from a number of vantage points and . . . each change in viewing can give rise to a change in interpretation of the scene." In L2 instruction, addressing these ideas with learners will make a difference to the way they understand choices available to them when turning their L1 thoughts into L2 output.

2.5.1 The Case of the Preterit versus the Imperfect in Spanish: Perspective at Work

Consider the sentence "She had short hair." A language like Spanish can construe this scene in either the imperfect or the preterit tenses, both simple pasts, yielding two options:

(1) *Ella **tenía** el pelo corto* (imperfect)
(2) *Ella **tuvo** el pelo corto* (preterit)

Examples like these generate a lot of confusion for learners of Spanish, and if there were a Top 5 of all-time difficult grammatical issues for the language, the double choice for the simple past would definitely be one of them. Certain pedagogical adaptations consider pragmatic aspects linked to usage contexts (*to describe in the past* or *to move a narrative forward*). Others focus on the tenses' discursive relationship with temporal markers, but a cognitive pedagogy emphasizes the symbolic relationship between the verb morphology and its semantics, which already includes lexical or pragmatic information – the idea is to train students to visualize that the ending -*ía* for the imperfect or -*ó* for the preterit carries the meaning by itself, regardless of context of use. ACL pedagogy avoids delivering a compendium of multiple rules and exceptions to the students and attempts, instead, to look at it like a matter of *perspective* via aspectual differences, where each tense conveys a different representation of an event from the past. These symbolic connections of form and meaning provide accessibility to understandable explanations that may lead to functional learning.[24] Figure 16a and 16b illustrate this idea with classroom materials for a prototype on each tense:

---

[24] See Niemeier (2013) for a cognitive-based analysis of the relationship between aspect and space, and Alonso-Aparicio & Llopis-García (2019) for an account of how this relationship applies to Spanish for theoretical and pedagogical purposes.

(a)

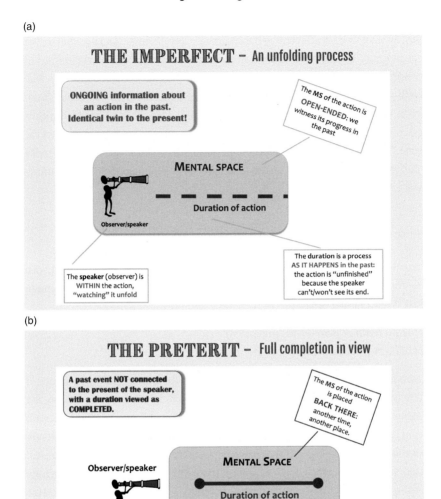

(b)

Figure 16(a) Teaching the Spanish imperfect, and
and (b) Teaching the Spanish preterit.

Returning to examples (1) and (2) above, Figure 17 helps visualize that verbal aspect expresses perspective in Spanish, and through aspect, speakers then convey their *vantage point* and whether that perspective toward the conceptual scenes is *global* or *local* in each example (Langacker 2008b: 11). The vantage point refers to

Figure 17 Visualizing the imperfect-preterit contrast in Spanish

the view of the speaker, which in this case is whether *having short hair* is seen with *closeness* (*inside* or locally for example 1) or with *distance* (*outside* or globally for example 2) from the specific stance that the speaker wishes to communicate.

For the imperfect, aspect creates a process that is unfolding in a local perspective, where the vantage point for the speaker/observer is situated *within* the mental space where the action takes place, watching it happen locally, "in real time.' The action has a duration that is considered to be "in progress" and the speaker cannot or will not "visualize" its beginning or end. The imperfect, in short, is the identical twin of the present tense, by which one can say "She **has** short hair" without needing to imply when the action starts or ends. It simply is and requires no further clarification, either because the duration of the action is not relevant, or because its ending is not in sight/known.

The prototype for the imperfect, then, is a network, presented in many textbooks as a mere list, that includes *description of an ongoing story, background information, descriptions in the past, reasons surrounding a main plot, habitual actions in the past,* etc. All these usages need not be unrelated, since the common thread between them all is that they offer a *local perspective*, meaning that they are viewed from *within* the mental space in which they unfold. In this manner, instead of presenting learners with a list of uses and contexts, the central meaning of INSIDE/local perspective can be the common denominator that relates them all.

The preterit, on the other hand, offers a "bird's-eye view" vantage point for the speaker/observer, who is now *outside* the mental space of the action. Because of this distance, the *global perspective* is independent from the mental space, and the action is regarded by the speaker in its entirety from another time and place. This depiction represents the perfect aspect of the tense, and the action is viewed as *completed* from beginning to end because of that distance.

In example (2), the speaker's communicative intent is that the short hair is no more – the time period of that hairstyle ended and even though it is not known to the interlocutors what she looks like now, what is clear, however, is that her hair is no longer short.

The prototype for the preterit connects textbook usages such as *specific actions finished in the past, succession of actions in the past, actions interrupted by other actions, clear temporal limits, repeated actions that are bounded by temporal markers*, etc. The global perspective and the mental distance of the speaker affords those usages a common thread and gives them all a connected meaning.

In the words of Llopis-García et al. (2012: 45. OT): "if we believe that any formal change in linguistic choice of words yields a semantic change, then the aim of grammatical instruction must be to provide the different values assigned to each form in order to understand how they alter the conveyed meaning." Prototype instruction links those values, not only for language practice, but to give students the agency to decide *what they mean* when they choose either verb. Ruiz & Torres (2022) offer a very similar perspective on the aspectual contrast, where they teach both tenses from a spatial perspective and situate the preterit *outside/fuera* of the speaker's narrative (example: *I studied* [1st Person. Preterit] *all afternoon yesterday*), while the imperfect places the speaker *inside/ dentro* the story (example: *When I was young, I spent* [1st Person.Imperfect] *every summer studying*). Figure 18 illustrates their examples, which also include temporal markers.

Figure 18 Perspective on the imperfect versus the preterit in Spanish

Applying the concept of perspective to a pedagogical prototype for the verbal system activates the semantics of each conjugation to convey an explicit representation of how speakers understand and choose to communicate events in the past. From this instructional approach, "linguistic meaning does not reside in the objective nature of the situation described but is crucially dependent on how the situation is apprehended" (Langacker 2008b: 11). Changes in communicative intent, speaker perspective, and personal stance will always mean changes in linguistic form, no matter the conceptual scene. Instruction can then shift to a *"depends on what you mean"* approach versus the more frequent *"this is the way [insert L2] works."*

2.6 Constructions

Construction grammar (CxG) (Goldberg 1995, 2003, 2006) is a long-established linguistic model, but the noted relevance of constructions (Cxs) in L2 Pedagogy is very recent, only from the last decade. As Gilquin and De Knop (2016: 4) point out, "second and foreign language [...] have not been the focus of many CxG-based studies so far." But there is much to be found here to contribute to the L2 classroom, and there is already a significant number of exciting ideas to positively impact what can be done in the L2 language classroom.

A construction, by definition, is a *unit* of language that is made out of *symbolic form-meaning pairings* and whose structure is *conventionalized by usage*. To understand what this means, let us deconstruct the definition:

- "Unit": Cxs can be combinations of morphemes, one-word items or many-word structures. Their versatility makes them especially interesting in the quest to recognize that language is inherently meaningful from the most basic to the most complex instantiations. When we attach an ending or suffix to a verb, we create tenses, like *-ed* for the past in English regular verbs, or *-aba/ía* in Spanish for the imperfect. Also, phrasal verbs or a caused-motion construction (like *boo someone off the stage*) count as such, as they "possess meanings that cannot be predicted from the parts in isolation" (Holme 2010a: 115). For the specific case of the learnability of phrasal verbs, Alejo-González (2010) points out that prepositions "are important to the construal of 'scenes,' especially in the basic domain of space, [and for] *semantic networks*, in which a basic or prototypical meaning gives rise to different semantic extensions" (p. 53). Figure 19 illustrates these points by way of motivating the phrasal verb *to look up to someone*, where the components *look, up,* or *to* have different meanings, but their combination by semantic extension becomes the completely new concept of *admiring someone.*

Figure 19 Motivating phrasal verbs in English

- "Symbolic form-meaning pairings": According to Goldberg (2006:3) "All levels of grammatical analysis involve constructions: learned pairings of form with semantic or discourse function, including morphemes or words, idioms, partially lexically filled and fully general phrasal patterns." This aligns with the CL view that language is meaningful and linguistic structure is motivated, arising from the context of human experience and conceptualization. From the stance of L2 pedagogy, additionally, considering the symbolic character of language means connecting with learners more effectively, "since it puts them in contact with recognizable, understandable and common aspects of their L1, which can also be transferred to the L2 to better overcome the initial barrier of understanding a new language" (Llopis-García 2009: 87. OT).

- "Conventionalized by use": This is an important part of the definition of Cx and key in understanding its value. Both constructivist and cognitive approaches to language hold the foundational principle that language is usage-based, which means that linguistic patterns represent conceptual scenes from human experience, and they emerge from repeated use by the speakers. Language learning in general, then, "occurs in relation to exposure to frequent patterns, and therefore the most recurrent chunks of language will be acquired earlier and faster" (Hijazo-Gascón & Llopis-García 2019: 7). This idea has enormous implications for L2 learning, because it contributes to the "de-foreignizing" of the L2 that was mentioned in Section 2.3.2. For L2 learners, working with usage-based input means that they will be able to encounter, identify, and process Cxs in real-life instances, which strongly supports the use of authentic materials in the class and prepares learners to understand linguistic notions in context.

Another way to define a construction is by using the metaphor of a picture, and in the words of Holme (2010a: 116):

> A representational picture consists of different signs. These might represent walls, a door, a roof and windows. These signs have only the individual significances just mentioned but together compose something more than the sum of their parts and represent a house. This "gestalt" is also evident in language. Just as the parts of the house can be recognized as combining into a single form so can those of a construction. Constructions are thus "cognitive" in two senses. First, they are "gestalt" in the sense just outlined. Second, their meaning reflects how cognition structures perception.

From the standpoint of existing literature, recent research (see Guilquin & De Knop 2016 and Boas 2022 for a complete overview) has shown that L2 learners do have mental representations of Cxs in their interlanguage, since they also have them in their L1. In L2, constructions will bring about language processing mechanisms that students already possess, and that help in making generalizations about the L2. Cxs, with their schematic structure, their semantic focus, and their generalizable nature, help understand linguistic structure, recognize its compositional pattern, and engage in meaningful production and creation. They empower learners in their understanding of "language as a whole,' with linguistic structures that are coherently related, instead of fragmentally learned through a scattered order of appearance in textbook chapters (Gras et al 2006). Mood selection in Romance languages is a good example of this, whereby the different uses of the subjunctive are not only taught in different chapters of a textbook (*describe people and objects, express wishes, communicate doubts,* etc.), but also across proficiency levels and never with a common semantic denominator. In the words of Ibarretxe-Antuñano & Cheikh-Khamis (2019: 117), "regardless of the specific lexical items involved in each particular utterance, ... constructional templates offer a motivated explanation of what the structures mean ..., and at the same time, they avoid possible 'exceptions to the rule' that may arise in specific instantiations."

Consider the following construction in English: [N+Ver], where N= noun, V= verb, and *-er* is an added morpheme to the verb, which actually turns the action into a noun with agency (for instance, a *maker* is an entity that makes something, or a *sharpener* is an entity that sharpens objects). From this schema, actual language can be created for words such as *pencil sharpener, party goer, money maker, man eater, conversation starter* ... and as many instances as the imagination allows, both conventional and novel.

Another example, this time from Spanish and the construction [A+INF], has *A* = the preposition *to* and INF = an infinitive (see Section 2.1). This Cx can be addressed at the A1 level, where students have very basic knowledge, but (similarly to what was discussed in Section 2.3) their first steps in recognizing and processing linguistic patterns are crucial. [A+INF] brings about the notion that constructions can have *open positions, closed positions,* or both. The latter refers to any part of a Cx that will always remain unchanged (the preposition *a* in our current Cx), whereas the former admits lexical variability and changes in every example (the INF here). The preposition *a* refers to a "forward motion toward a destination or goal" that can be metaphorically conceptualized as "having an end goal in mind." The fictive motion of the preposition can be conceptualized with the metaphor INTENTION IS FORWARD MOTION, whereas the infinitive, understood as "the idea of an action," will become the end goal. Thus, in Spanish, any call to action can be built with this Cx: *a trabajar* (an entreaty to work)*, a comer* (a call to eat)*, a dormir* (a command to go to sleep), etc. Figure 20 illustrates the Cx.

Working with the closed position of this Cx promotes chunking and a sense of linguistic stability from accessing "formulaic sequences ... that provide [the students] with data which is analysed and fed into their grammatical development" (Ellis & Shintani 2014: 72). This kind of chunking is important from the A1 level onwards (Section 3.1.1) and will assist in the identification of the Cx as a whole, in order to ultimately help with the internalization of the pattern.

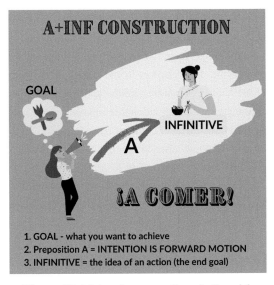

Figure 20 A1-level constructions in Spanish

- Addressing the closed position as unchanging enables students to recognize the pattern across texts, which will help enormously in the long run, since all instances of prepositions followed by verbs in Spanish will use infinitives, and this particular Cx is just one example of that larger pattern (Llopis-García 2021a).
- Addressing the open position gives learners space for lexical creativity, as it "can help students come to grips with Cxs as productive meanings that are built around one or more fixed items" (Holme 2010a: 122). Targeting learner confidence, they get to hypothesize about what may or may not work, enabling L2 intralinguistic reasoning. Working "with constructions that are partially schematic and partially lexically specified . . . has the advantage that it is easy to understand and simple to remember" (Herbst 2016: 40–41).

On this last thought, there is another undeniable advantage, and it is the reduction of metalanguage when dealing with grammar points (see Section 5.2.1). Many L2 students, beyond the natural difficulties of a new and different linguistic system, struggle with the terminology that often accompanies it: *dative, direct object pronoun, conjunction, subordinate clause, gerund, the subjunctive, subject and predicate* . . . These are just a few examples of what learners who may not come from an L1 educational background on syntax or morphology must contend with. But they have all kinds of backgrounds, learn L2s for as many different reasons as there are learners themselves, and the goal of their communicative competence may or may not be based on academic achievement or functional knowledge. Both ACL and CxG bring a decrease in metalanguage as a welcome alternative for diverse classroom settings and learning goals.

Verbs of emotion in Spanish (also known as psych-verb Cxs), for instance, are built on the schema of *Object + Verb + Subject* in traditional instruction. Figure 21 teaches with an *Experiencer*, an *Action,* and a *Performer/Idea* as more accessible alternatives to understanding the representational roles of linguistic elements, focusing less on students being able to identify grammatical metalanguage, which may not be the focus of their learning goals (Section 5.2.1 will return to this issue).

Herbst (2016: 38) defends the use of the term *construction* "as a relatively neutral and non-committal cover term" which reduces the complexity of what is taught and helps learners focus on form-meaning pairings without the additional hurdle of terminology. He proposes *V-ing constructions* for different uses of the gerund, the *going to construction* for the future continuous, and points out that "awkward form-function mix-ups such as that of 'adjectives used as nouns' can easily be avoided by identifying a *the_ADJ construction* . . . to refer to a group of people: Some people think *the rich* should pay more tax" (p. 40).

Figure 21 The psych-verb construction in Spanish

All examples provided from English and Spanish show how meaningful learning is encouraged. Pedagogical interventions may include:

- Bringing a list of examples to class and having students match the Cxs to their meanings
- Creating a list of examples with the students, empowering them to be creative with the target language, and discussing their creations for meaningful practice. This promotes student agency for risk-taking in new productions and a more "dare to do," enjoyable approach to vocabulary and grammar learning
- Reading authentic texts and having students identify instances of the Cx, helping them to further understand their meaning by seeing it in context. This strategy can reinforce the mental *constructicon* of the students, where the schematic Cxs are stored and become more readily accessible for production (see Section 3.2.2 for ideas on how to do this)
- Helping learners focus on form to create grammatically sound input and empower their sense of fluency (and thus their affective bond with the L2), because "correct usage is itself promoted by conscious processes of exploration" (Holme 2010b: 373).

Regarding the level at which constructions should be addressed, although voices in the field point toward the advanced levels (Ruiz de Mendoza & Llach 2016; Gonzálvez-García 2019), a study with English phrasal verbs shows evidence that "it is at the intermediate level, that of the structural patterns, that learners seem to be the most successful and thus, presumably, have best internalized the construction" (Guilquin & De Knop 2016: 5). I will posit here, however, and with evidence from empirical research (Suárez-Campos 2020), that from the A1 level, training students to work with usage-based, motivated, spatial, and metaphorical approaches is not only advisable, but also absolutely necessary if linguists and researchers want empirical studies to assess learning in environments where there has been a genuine engagement with ACL principles (see Section 5). Consistent ACL instruction from the start will enable research on ACL interventions to be more insightful, since "the nature of knowledge underlying expert behavior depends on experience or systematic practice" (Alonso-Aparicio, 2014: 24. OT). If classroom-based research is to reliably assess ACL, it must go hand in hand with the daily pedagogical practice of the language courses. The more "expert" students become at ACL-based learning, the easier it will be for researchers to design and implement materials that result in learners engaging with and internalizing ACL principles (Martín-Gascón et al 2023).

2.7 Final Considerations

So far, the foundational concepts of CL and how they relate to the teaching and learning of grammar and lexis have been outlined and explained. Additionally, examples of pedagogical applications and classroom materials have been pro-vided, alongside explanations of why they are useful and should be brought to the language classroom.

The following sections delve deeper into considerations for material design, together with additional teaching materials for the Spanish/L2 classroom that can be used as a stepping stone for designing and creating alternatives in other languages. Insights on teaching methodologies that already have a widespread presence in L2 settings and how they merge well with ACL approaches will also be addressed.

3 Methodological Aspects and Resources

At the beginning of this volume, I mentioned that although the field of SLA has made important contributions to the field of L2 teaching, a significant number of studies and publications have not had the desired impact or a lasting influence for the teaching community. This section aims to gather some of the theoretical considerations from SLA that provide valuable knowledge and best practices for L2 Pedagogy that are compatible with ACL approaches.

3.1 L2 Methodology and ACL

Doughty & Long (2003), Lee & VanPatten (2003), Hinkel (2005, 2011), Housen and Pierrard (2005), Gass and Mackey (2012), or Ellis and Shintani (2014) are excellent works that address all issues pertaining to SLA and that explore the intersection of the field with L2 pedagogy. It is from Ellis and Shintani (2014: 22–27) that we extract three SLA-based criteria that have direct and empirically proven effectiveness in L2 language teaching, and that have a valuable and direct relationship with cognitive-based approaches: formulaic expressions, focus on meaning,[25] and focus on form.

3.1.1 Formulaic Expressions

These are sequences of language that speakers learn "as a whole" and that at the moment of apprehension are not analyzed grammatically, nor understood by their individual components. These types of expressions are very diverse and may happen at all levels of language acquisition (both in L1 and L2). Some examples, for instance, are the conversation starter *How are you doing?*, the constructional chunk *Looking forward to V+ing,* or the discourse marker *By the way.*

Chunks are a type of formulaic expression that can be defined as ready-made lexical items. They are very productive in the L2 classroom because they give learners (at any level) a sense of fluency. Especially at the beginner levels, chunks enable "the speaker to attend to other aspects of communication and to plan larger pieces of discourse, which would naturally facilitate fluent language production under real-time conditions" (Dörnyei 2013:162). It is important, however, to teach them explicitly, because as Pérez-Serrano (2018) points out, "awareness raising is not enough and should be supplemented by form-focused instruction, including manipulating the input to direct learners' attention . . . and facilitating more explicit activities to promote intentional learning" (p. 133). In this sense, chunks can also relate to the constructivist approach to grammar and vocabulary in ACL (see Section 2.6 and also Section 2.3 on Metaphor and Metaphorical Competence for more insights on the value of formulaic expressions.). As seen earlier, the "call for action" construction [A+infinitive] in Spanish (Figure 20), with its closed and open positions can be a high-yielding pick to create productive fluency among students and help them engage with the language "in their own terms."

3.1.2 Focus on Form

"Not only are many grammatical meaning-form relationships low in salience but they can also be redundant in the understanding of the meaning of an utterance." This quote by Ellis (2008: 388) summarizes the main issue with the teaching of grammar in L2, and the work of VanPatten (1996, 2004, 2015) and colleagues

---

[25] However, since any ACL-based approach to grammar and lexis *is already* focused on meaning and meaning-making as a foundational principle (as the focus of this *Element* shows), there will be no additions to this criterion beyond its mention.

(Benati & Lee 2015) on *Processing Instruction* (a type of focus on form instruction) provides ample theoretical and empirical support for this claim.

Focus on form instruction (Long 1991; Long & Robinson 1998) argues that just because a grammatical structure may be present in the input learners are exposed to, there are no guarantees that it will be "picked up" for further processing. This is especially true for the two conditions underlined in the quote by Ellis: "saliency" and "redundancy" are two major issues that affect the processing of grammatical content. In Spanish/L2, there is no better example of this issue – and several others – than the subjunctive mood (Llopis-García 2009, 2010, 2019a). The pedagogical difficulty of this structure is addressed in the following example, which shows the subjunctive verb underlined and in boldface:

*Estoy buscando cualquier apartamento que **tenga** dos dormitorios y dos baños*
(*I am looking for any apartment that **has** two bedrooms and two bathrooms*)

a) As we can see, the subjunctive belongs in the realm of subordination. This means that its position within a sentence is usually relegated to the middle, with its saliency thus compromised due to the amount of lexical and grammatical information that precedes and follows its presence. Research with processing instruction shows that students process elements in the initial position of a statement first, continuing with those that are at the end, with the greatest difficulty to those in the central (or middle) position (VanPatten 1996, 2004, 2015).

b) In the example above, both *I am looking for (estoy buscando)* and *any (cualquier)* convey the semantic information of an unidentified apartment (Section 4.2.1). So when the subjunctive, which also codes non-identifications comes about, its communicative value is rendered redundant because "there are other forms in the input with greater semantic value that, under equal processability conditions, have greater chances of being detected" (Llopis-García 2019a: 257. OT). *Tenga*, then (as grammatical form versus the lexical unit *cualquier*), will have less of a chance to be processed as intake because it is simply perceived as less meaningful or not perceived at all.

Given these issues, focus on form (FonF) aims to establish a cognitive relationship between learner and linguistic form, thus allowing a processing based more on perception and comprehension, and less on memorization.[26] It indicates "a concern with the structural system of language from a communicative perspective"

---

[26] There will always be a degree of memorization and "studying" of lexical-grammatical concepts. This is due to the exam-based configuration of many L2 courses, not only in academic, K-12, or higher education contexts, but also in order to obtain competence-by-level official certifications.

(Dörnyei 2013: 159) and directs the attention of the learner to a problematic grammatical feature so that it can be noticed first, processed second, and finally incorporated into working memory for comprehension and ready-retrieval in production. Cadierno (2008b) and, more recently, Nassaji (2016) provide a compilation of research studies that since the early 1980s and well into the 2010s provide solid evidence in favor of this methodology. Figure 22 (adapted from Llopis-García 2009) shows a classroom-based example of what a FonF activity looks like (most specifically, from a processing instruction perspective).

In this activity (See section 4.2.1 for a complete explanation of the ID☺/ non-ID☺ prototype for mood selection and the emoji associated with each mood), designed to direct the learner's attention to a form-meaning connection of the indicative/subjunctive selection in relative clauses, tennis player Rafael Nadal and his (potential) new home are the main characters of the prompt, which asks students to read the sentences and decide whether they mean that

FOCUS ON FORM
RELATIVE CLAUSES WITH MOOD SELECTION

RAFA NADAL'S HOUSE 🏠

Tennis star Rafa Nadal talks about his new home in an interview. (1) What would he say if he has already bought it? (*Ya comprada*) (2) And what if he hasn't bought it yet? (*Aún no*) Indicate with ✅ whether he already has it or not:

Rafa habla de una casa que...

	YA COMPRADA	AÚN NO
tiene una terraza grande	____	____
tenga muchas ventanas	____	____
esté cerca de un centro comercial	____	____
está en una playa privada	____	____
sea bonita y agradable	____	____
es moderna y original	____	____
cuesta más de 500,000 €	____	____
cueste menos de 500,000 €	____	____
transmita buenas vibraciones	____	____
transmite paz y serenidad	____	____

Figure 22 An example of a focus on form grammar activity

a house is already in his possession (an ID🔲 of the house), or whether, on the contrary, he hasn't bought it yet (a non-ID🔲 of the house). As the image shows, the main clause of the subordination has been highlighted above, since it is equal for all examples provided. That, in turn, places the main verb of the subordinate clause in first position and facilitates the focus of the students on the verb. The classification of the sentences according to their meaning (*Ya comprada = already bought = ID🔲* versus *Aún no = not yet = non-ID🔲* rests solely on the interpretation of the subordinate verbs. Any other repetitive or semantically equivalent information has been eliminated, and the semantic value of the whole sentence is, every time, provided by the subordinate verb alone. This is very clearly specified in one of the examples, where both sentences are exactly the same and only the verb ending -*a*/-*e* provides the information to understand that each describes a different scenario:

Main clause: *Rafa habla de una casa que . . . (Rafa talks about a house that . . .)*
Subordinate clause: ***cuesta***🔲*/**cueste**🔲 500,000€ (**costs** 500,000€)*

FonF has proven to be a very useful method for the teaching and learning of complex grammatical structures, and it is widely known and used in textbook materials (VanPatten et al. 2012; Alonso Raya et al. 2021). Piquer-Píriz and Boers (2019) make an interesting point when they say that formal contexts of instruction, as opposed to natural or immersive settings, only afford a limited amount of time of exposure to the L2, which also provides less opportunity for interaction and for meaningful use of the target language. FonF proposes an approach to grammar that is based on the symbolic nature of form and meaning (structured to allow understanding without additional or other semantically redundant linguistic elements), while ACL enables connections between those forms and their meanings (by presenting challenging grammatical topics via prototypical distinctions, as in the example above). See Figure 23[27] for another example with a form-meaning-image match.

Cadierno (2008: 264) summarizes this symbiosis: "The type of grammar teaching embodied in the focus-on-form approach, with its key focus on form and meaning relations . . . is thus more in consonance with the language view advocated by cognitive linguistics, and is expected to benefit from its insights." Two longitudinal studies that combined ACL and FonF offer empirical evidence for this view: Llopis-García (2010) for the teaching of mood selection in Spanish to German learners, and Colasacco (2019) for the teaching of deictic motion verbs in Spanish to German and Italian learners.

---

[27] *Me molesta tu actitud* translates to *Your attitude bothers me* (Martín-Gascón, Llopis-García, & Alonso-Aparicio, 2023).

Figure 23 An example of focus on form with image pairing

A Short Note on FonF and Gamification

Larsen-Freeman (2015: 265) reports on many research studies that evaluate not only the historical efficacy of grammar in the classroom, but also attitudes of both teachers and students across languages. She states that "the main findings suggest that grammar instruction is perceived by both students and teachers as necessary and effective, but not something they enjoy doing." Langacker (2008a: 78) also describes grammar practice in the language classroom as "the soulless internalization of arbitrary restrictions." To challenge these appreciations, Section 4 will include examples from tools used for digital and visual content creation, but on the topic of a form-focused approach to grammar, the concept of *gamification*, understood as "the incorporation of approaches, procedures and dynamics typical of game-play in the learning of L2" (Román-Mendoza 2018: 24. OT), offers interesting potential for engaging and motivating language practice in instructional settings. The beginning of the COVID-19 pandemic in 2020 saw the forced rise of online instruction, and the use of technology in the classroom stopped being optional for most. Among the many already existing apps and digital tools for online engagement, Kahoot! (an app for gamified learning) was one of them. The combination of ACL-grammar with FonF and multimodal, interactive, and gamified approaches to assess/review classroom content can provide a unique learning experience

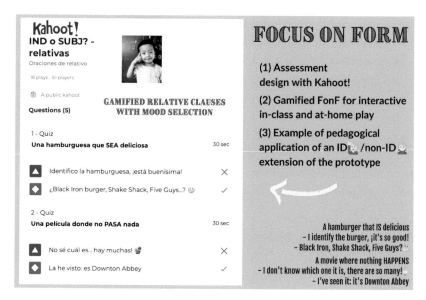

Figure 24 An example of gamified focus on form

aimed at better content retention and understanding, both in class and at home. In line with the prototypical approach to mood selection featured in this section, Figure 24 shows a preview of a Kahoot! activity for relative clauses with indicative or subjunctive in a B1-level Spanish course.

Through activities like these, the L2 instructor can check student understanding of the target forms in a low-stakes assessment situation that motivates a play-to-learn approach to grammar. This type of interactive task engages learners to participate in a fun, healthy, competitive manner while also focusing on the grammatical form at hand. And because FonF encourages the reduction of linguistic information that can carry the same semantic value and render it redundant, the length of the prompt is made shorter and easier to process under the time constraints of the game.

3.2 Lexical Approaches[28] to ACL Vocabulary

Being a competent user of an L2 is not only about having linguistic knowledge. It is also essential to be in tune with all the elements that intervene in language use so that the message is effective and appropriate both to the interlocutor and to the context in which it happens. This could be a definition of *Communicative*

---

[28] For a comprehensive overview and understanding of what these approaches bring to language learning and teaching and their compatibility with cognitive classrooms, the reading of the following sources is recommended: Lewis 1997; Boers and Lindstromberg 2008, 2009; Schmitt 2008 (in English); as well as Higueras 2006, 2011; and Pérez-Serrano 2017 (in Spanish).

Competence, which is essentially about knowing words, what they mean, how to combine them, and when to use them.

About words in L2 instruction, the teaching and learning of vocabulary is at the top of the list of pedagogical priorities. In many market-ready textbooks, every chapter or unit gathers the relevant vocabulary in the final pages, dividing the lexical input into linguistic categories (i.e. *nouns*, *verbs*, *adjectives*, *other expressions*). However, teaching vocabulary is a much more complex endeavor than compilations and lists of words at the end of every chapter or session. Instruction that takes lexical approaches into account (and fits well with ACL approaches), according to Aristu and Torres (2021), follows these guidelines:

- Lexical units are featured systematically and are an end in themselves (not the means to learn something else). They are constantly being recycled and reused in different types of tasks throughout the textbook or content planning
- Attention to vocabulary that is contextualized in a meaningful manner through different kinds of texts (aural, written, interactive, etc.)
- Lexical units, lexical chunks, collocations, and frequent combinations are addressed in every unit so that words are not learned in isolation or as a list; This is also consistent with what Goldberg (2006) expressed in her definition of what a construction is, where "patterns are stored as constructions even if they are fully predictable as long as they occur with sufficient frequency" (p. 5)
- Vocabulary learning is highlighted through the use of special fonts, colors, animations, or images that allow for embodied awareness, noticing, and processing of the linguistic forms
- Lexical structures and constructions are taught with specific techniques, such as association (for attention to morphology and collocational traits), translation (for attention to representational, motivational, and cultural features), or metaphorical uses (for attention to embodied understanding of the target language).

In ACL-based approaches to lexis, the grouping of lexical items is still a valid option, but on the condition that it reflects the relationships and types of combinations that the mental *lexicon* allows. There are some pedagogical techniques that are especially apt when working from this perspective. Three of them combine well with cognitive ideas: mind maps, mapped-out texts, and work with collocations.

3.2.1 Mind Maps

Mind maps have always been present in L2 classrooms since the communicative approach became the norm in L2 pedagogy in the late twentieth century, given that their visual and relational aspects facilitate access to meaningful

Figure 25 A collaborative mind map in Spanish B1

generation, visualization, structure, and classification of ideas (Contreras et al. 2019; Sans Baulenas et al. 2017, 2021; García Sánchez et al. 2018, to name but a few textbooks that make constant use of them). These maps are very effective in improving synthesis and memorization skills, since they help learners develop a thought or idea through their own processing and organization of newly learned content (Aristu & Torres 2021: 10. OT). In an ACL-based classroom, mind maps become another pedagogical ally to emphasize that language is symbolic, as well as the saliency of embodiment and the semantic extensions that arise from prototypes. Mind maps can also assist when approaching the closed positions of constructions, helping students chart related meanings or craft road maps of creative L2 production that stem from an unchanging piece of language (See Figure 29 in Section 3.2.3).

Figure 25 and the footnote[29] shows an actual classroom example from a B1-level Spanish class where, at the end of the unit, students created a mind map of all relevant vocabulary they had learned, plus additional examples they came up with by way of work with Cxs. In L2 courses that emphasize ACL concepts such as space, embodiment, sensorimotor experience, categorization, or MC, it is fitting to use mind maps that are done collaboratively, with some students providing examples and others offering collocations, relational links, or related terms, thus empowering each other to think creatively and focus on meaning-making. Also, while the textbook of the course may provide a traditional list of vocabulary with words and their translations, the map from Figure 25 facilitated a creative spin for learners to connect lexical units, since it is "not just about learning thousands of words and their different meanings,

---

[29] The theme of the unit was BUSINESS (LOS NEGOCIOS), so this mind map draws on topics such as *industry, banking, money, goods and storage, demand or supply*, etc.

but also about perceiving lexical combinations and relationships" (Piquer-Píriz & Boers 2019: 55. OT). Last, while these are ideas and pedagogical content that can be found in non-ACL classrooms, an instruction that constantly emphasizes the symbolic nature of language and the motivation of words yields classroom experiences like the one in Figure 25, where students went beyond what was required, as they brought forward their own personal interests and ideas to develop their "personal lexis"[30] and contribute to collective knowledge. These learning outcomes are consistent with what ACL can bring to the language classroom, highlighting its compatibility with many commonly used pedagogical techniques.

Another example in English is provided in Figure 26, which shows vocabulary on the topic of JOBS. Here, linguistic categories group the words without explicit metalanguage (*actions* instead of *verbs*; *descriptions* instead of *adjectives*) and in relational combinations (*give someone a job, low-paying job, rewarding* or *interesting job,* etc.), prompting meaningful engagement with the content and the development of phraseological and metaphorical competences.

Further ACL-based instruction (in collaboration or individually) with this material may include:

- Developing conceptual fluency (Lantolf & Bobrova 2014):
  - Asking students to produce their own examples based on the provided material

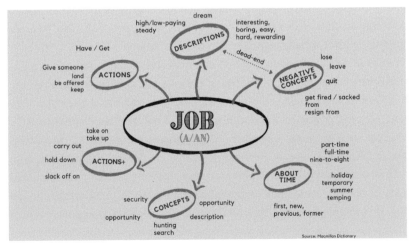

Figure 26 A mind map around the concept of JOB

---

[30] Vocabulary that allows every person to represent themselves and their reality linguistically (Troitiño 2017: 148–149).

- ○ Requesting that students explain, in their own words, the meaning of certain collocations or phrasal verbs.
- ○ Enabling an online search for examples and asking students to explain their findings
- ○ Asking students to give examples related to content in the map in order to check for meaningful understanding of the content. A variation is to group students to come up with their own questions to ask to other groups. Examples of this include: *What is an example of a high-paying job for you? / Under what circumstances would you quit your job? / What can you do if you're job hunting?*
- • Contributing to symbolic awareness and constructional understanding of the language by:
  - ○ Bringing a text to class and prompting them to find the lexical units from the map (see Section 3.2.2 on **Mapped-out Texts**)
  - ○ Creating activities to match the lexical units of the map with their meaning (see Section 4 for interactive activities).

Pérez-Serrano (2017: 8. OT) explains that "lexical-semantic competence is understood transversally, since it has components from both linguistic, socio-linguistic and pragmatic competence, while also referring to declarative, pro-cedural and strategic knowledge." Mind maps and the above proposed activities are aimed at fostering this competence. Additionally, they provide the space to develop metaphorical competence and focus on semantic networks, as well as on semantic and constructional aspects of lexis.

3.2.2 Mapped-Out Texts

This technique, with a growing pedagogical trend since the end of the 2010s and with expanding popularity due to the rise of online teaching during the COVID-19 pandemic, is used to help students notice and engage with meaningful fragments of a text because of their linguistic value.

By mapping texts, learner agency is developed because it allows engagement with a text in order to figure out what fragments are meaningful based on their contextual, metaphorical, morphological, constructional, collocational or gram-matical value. Students assign this value from prompts and upon comprehen-sion of the content. Texts from the textbook or those chosen by instructors, audio/video transcripts, and even the black/smartboards of the classrooms themselves can be mapped out (Aristu 2020). From these interactions with texts, the so-called incidental learning that happens when students engage in reading becomes explicit and therefore intentional.

The way to map out a text is: (a) by giving precise instructions on *what to map*: verbs with their prepositions, discourse markers, frequent word combinations from mind maps, prepositions, idiomatic/figurative expressions, etc.; and (b) by instituting a coding mechanism for the text: color highlights, boldface, underlining, placing an emoji next to the item, cutting and pasting into a table in another document, etc. Any lexical combination can be the focus of the mapping activity, in what Lewis (1993) calls "pedagogical chunking".

Figure 27 (next page), shows a B2-level course of Spanish where students worked collaboratively in a *Google Doc* to map out a journalistic text according to the following categories (two assigned per group): *verbal constructions in the present/in the future/in the past, relative constructions, connectors of transition/to add additional information/other kinds*, and *constructions of interest to you*.

The pedagogical goal of this mapped-out text was to review two main grammatical topics that had been studied from a cognitive perspective: tense and mood selection (see Section 2.5.1 for the simple pasts and Sections 3.2.1 and 4.2.1 on *focus on form* for mood selection and its prototype) and discourse markers, both a major focus of the course for the development of discursive competence. Each group was assigned a tense (which included mood as well) and a connector category (i.e. *verbal constructions in the present + connectors of transition*). The category of relative constructions was considered part of the connector family, and *expressions of interest* was added as a "bonus category" for the students to add to their personal lexis. The collaborative aspect of the mapping allowed students to verbalize ideas about the grammatical and discursive aspects, as well as to engage directly with the text in search of the target constructions, seeing them in context and analyzing how they worked or with what they collocated.

Another example of a mapped-out text is again on the subject of discourse markers, but at the B1 level. In this activity,[31] students wrote a paragraph each on time management issues they faced in their day-to-day college lives. Once they wrote their text, it was assigned to another student, who had to highlight connectors and markers for cohesion in yellow (i.e. linguistic competence), plus lexical-grammatical constructions that stood out for their quality in boldface (i.e. personal lexis development and the highlighting of items that had been previously studied from embodiment, perspective, or motivation). Finally, students read all contributions and awarded five stars to those they considered to be best built (Figure 28 on page 58 shows an excerpt from the whole board).

---

[31] https://padlet.com/RLLG/C13conectoresytiempo

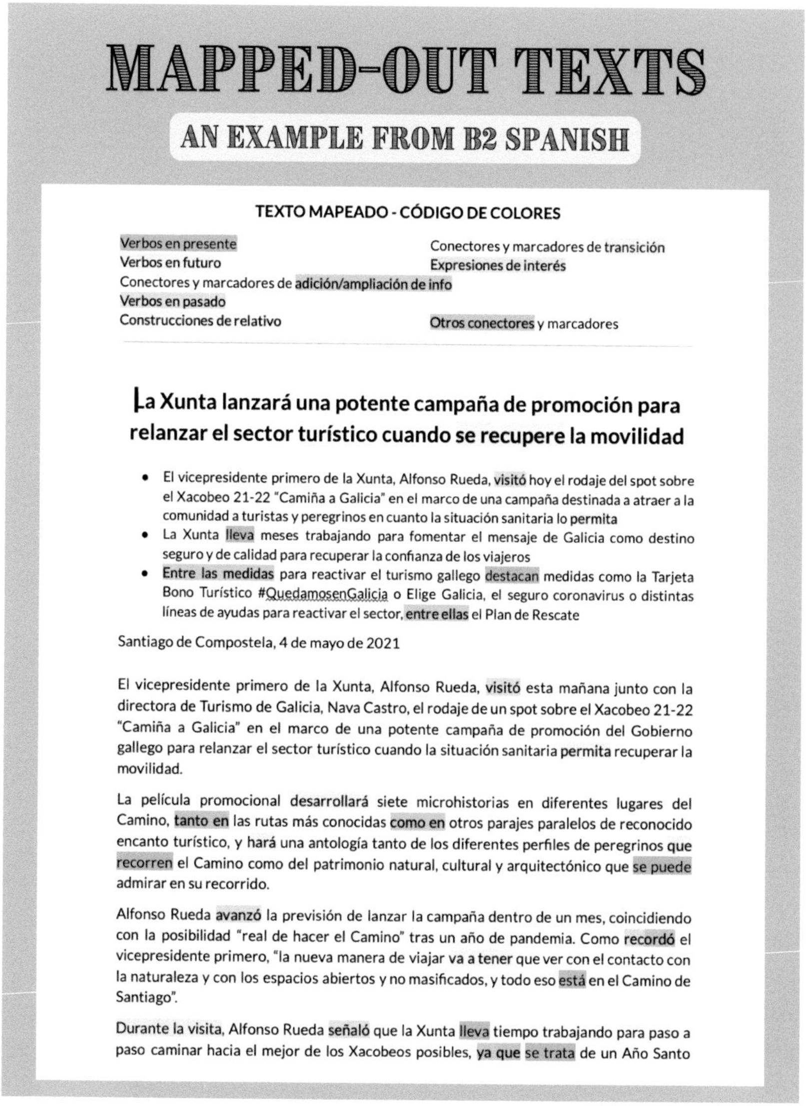

MAPPED-OUT TEXTS

AN EXAMPLE FROM B2 SPANISH

TEXTO MAPEADO - CÓDIGO DE COLORES

Verbos en presente
Verbos en futuro
Conectores y marcadores de adición/ampliación de info
Verbos en pasado
Construcciones de relativo
Conectores y marcadores de transición
Expresiones de interés
Otros conectores y marcadores

La Xunta lanzará una potente campaña de promoción para relanzar el sector turístico cuando se recupere la movilidad

- El vicepresidente primero de la Xunta, Alfonso Rueda, visitó hoy el rodaje del spot sobre el Xacobeo 21-22 "Camiña a Galicia" en el marco de una campaña destinada a atraer a la comunidad a turistas y peregrinos en cuanto la situación sanitaria lo permita
- La Xunta lleva meses trabajando para fomentar el mensaje de Galicia como destino seguro y de calidad para recuperar la confianza de los viajeros
- Entre las medidas para reactivar el turismo gallego destacan medidas como la Tarjeta Bono Turístico #QuedamosenGalicia o Elige Galicia, el seguro coronavirus o distintas líneas de ayudas para reactivar el sector, entre ellas el Plan de Rescate

Santiago de Compostela, 4 de mayo de 2021

El vicepresidente primero de la Xunta, Alfonso Rueda, visitó esta mañana junto con la directora de Turismo de Galicia, Nava Castro, el rodaje de un spot sobre el Xacobeo 21-22 "Camiña a Galicia" en el marco de una potente campaña de promoción del Gobierno gallego para relanzar el sector turístico cuando la situación sanitaria permita recuperar la movilidad.

La película promocional desarrollará siete microhistorias en diferentes lugares del Camino, tanto en las rutas más conocidas como en otros parajes paralelos de reconocido encanto turístico, y hará una antología tanto de los diferentes perfiles de peregrinos que recorren el Camino como del patrimonio natural, cultural y arquitectónico que se puede admirar en su recorrido.

Alfonso Rueda avanzó la previsión de lanzar la campaña dentro de un mes, coincidiendo con la posibilidad "real de hacer el Camino" tras un año de pandemia. Como recordó el vicepresidente primero, "la nueva manera de viajar va a tener que ver con el contacto con la naturaleza y con los espacios abiertos y no masificados, y todo eso está en el Camino de Santiago".

Durante la visita, Alfonso Rueda señaló que la Xunta lleva tiempo trabajando para paso a paso caminar hacia el mejor de los Xacobeos posibles, ya que se trata de un Año Santo

Figure 27 A collaborative mapped-out text in B2 Spanish

All learning objectives presented in the activities from Figures 27 and 28 are in synchrony with ACL pedagogy, because they "encourage learners to wonder why certain words collocate, how the meaning of an idiom is connected to its original use, how different uses of a word are interrelated, and so on" (Boers 2013: 219). Additionally, the usefulness of mapped-out texts matches various ACL purposes. For instance, students become aware of the symbolic nature of language, that is, the association between linguistic forms/Cxs and their

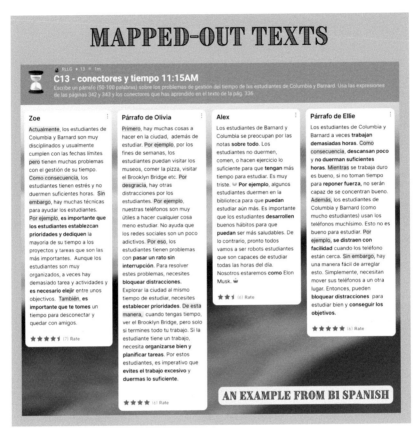

Figure 28 Mapped-out connectors and personal lexis in B1 Spanish

meaning. This technique also presents lexical units in context, situated from a usage-based perspective, which goes beyond traditional glossary lists or tables. Finally, depending on the prompt, awareness on the communicative, linguistic, and metaphorical functions of chunks, units, or constructions can be fostered.

3.2.3 Collocations

Philip (2011: 3), in line with cognitive views, observes that "meaning is ... realised by words in combinations, each single word relying on its neighbours to stabilise the overall message being conveyed." In this sense, *collocations* are chunks that frequently co-occur together in the input. For the purpose of L2 teaching, under the umbrella of collocations two types of combinations can be recognized: grammatical combinations (such as verbs and their prepositions, where for instance, the preposition *from* will often be found alongside the verb *choose*) and lexical combinations (like when the adverb *vitally* is frequently found in combination with *important*).

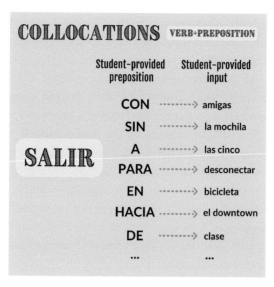

Figure 29 Collocations with student input in A1 Spanish

The sections on mapped-out texts and mind maps have already covered a number of ways in which collocational work engages learners with symbolic units. Collocations also draw specific attention to linguistic features that are hard to notice or to process, such as the highly polysemous prepositions and their combination with verbs. Figure 29[32] (above) provides a classroom activity with A1 students, where the instructor provides a motion verb like *salir/exit* and students contribute prepositions to hypothesize whether they work in combination with the verb. Once it has been determined that a number of prepositions do, in fact, collocate with the verb and, in fact again, change the meaning of the motion and its direction, new input is requested from the learners: a completion of the collocation with any lexical items that may settle the meaning of the whole expression.

An activity like this is of particular importance when addressing motion events in typologically different languages, like English and Spanish (Talmy 2000; Cadierno 2008b; Ibarretxe-Antuñano & Hijazo-Gascón 2015; Hijazo-Gascón 2021). Aguiló-Mora & Negueruela-Azarola (2015: 74) point out that "describing trajectories and motion through a new language is conceptually challenging since choosing what to foreground is conditioned by the L1." This is conceptually harder than it seems, and when a basic-level task like *Giving directions* comes about, the challenges multiply because "learners are dealing with the construction of space, motion, trajectories, and directionality in two

---

[32] The resulting phrases are: LEAVING *con/with friends, sin/without the backpack, a/at five o'clock, para/in order to unplug, en/on a bycicle, hacia/toward downtown, de/from class.*

different, conceptually opposite ways by changing their L1 thinking patterns to provide directions in their L2" (also see Talmy 2000 for a complete description of typology and Slobin 1996 for further information on the concept of *Thinking for speaking*). The work from Figure 29 can contribute to the saliency of Spanish motion verbs, which conflate trajectory but not manner, while the English counterpart conveys manner but requires a satellite (a preposition) to express trajectory (*out*). An example of this is the contrast between *subir corriendo/to run up*, where *subir* conveys the upward trajectory and the gerund *corriendo/running* provides the manner of the motion. English, on the other hand, provides the manner in the verb, *to run*, while the trajectory rests with the preposition (also called a *satellite* in typology). This distinction can be very confusing for speakers of both languages, so explicit work with grammatical collocations can help raise learner awareness and engagement with Cxs of motion for better chances of intake.

Another example,[33] as seen in Figure 30, offers work with lexical collocations on the topic of TIME MANAGEMENT with the activity design tool *learningapps.org* (Section 4). In this exercise, students can review collocations learned during previous classwork and self-check their recall ability by completing the full expression: *dedicate time to something, manage time well, hours of rest*, etc.

Figure 30 Activity design on collocations

---

[33] https://learningapps.org/view20196836

3.3 Final Considerations

Collocations, mind maps, and mapped-out texts are pedagogical practices compatible with ACL approaches because they all focus on promoting form-and-meaning fluency in L2. With these tools, work with linguistic motivation becomes more accessible because Cxs are seen in context, like the usage-based perspective of authentic materials in the mapped-out text option of Figure 27. Motivation can also be easily worked into a mind map that addresses a prototype and then its semantic extensions via metaphorical links. This process may be more memorable (and enjoyable) than looking up words and their translations at the end of a textbook chapter. Plus, "learners who are aware that an L2 is much more than a system of arbitrary form-meaning connections may be relatively likely to adopt mnemonically fruitful practices of insightful learning rather than less effective ones associated with blind memorisation" (Boers & Lindstromberg 2008: 18).

Finally, as part of a professional development course on Cognitive Linguistic Approaches to Grammar and Lexis that I teach every year to teachers of Spanish/L2, this checklist on "cognitive lexis" is designed for language instructors who want to create their own ACL content. Figure 31 (see p. 62) provides this material and the next section dives deeper into the topic of pedagogical design.

4 Cognitive Pedagogical Design

4.1 Educational Technology and L2

Because our daily lives now incorporate mobile technology and the ubiquitous presence of social media, the L2 language classroom has tremendous potential for methodological improvement both in synchronous or asynchronous settings, as well as in face-to-face, hybrid, or online learning environments. There are cognitive, pedagogical, and learning opportunities that technology affords in education in general, and in L2 in particular (Farr & Murray 2016; Malinowski & Kern 2016; Alejaldre-Biel 2018, Rocca 2018, Román Mendoza 2018; Aristu & Torres 2021).

For the particular case of ACL, there is a recurrent call about the need to develop pedagogy-effective teaching materials in order to make them as mainstream and readily available as possible to both instructors and students (Tyler 2008; Boers 2011, 2013; Nacey 2017, Tyler, Huang & Jan 2018; Suárez-Campos, Hijazo-Gascón, & Ibarretxe-Antuñano 2020; Luo 2021; Martín-Gascón et al., 2023). With educational technology ready to facilitate the hurdles of content building, the visual and representational nature of grammar/lexis is within reach and easier than ever.

COGNITIVE LEXIS

Use this list of ideas to check your work as you create materials. You do not have to apply all these criteria at once. It will depend on what teaching objectives you want to address in every activity you design.

☐ Is there linguistic **motivation**? Meaning: can you explain the experiential, embodied origin of the lexical item?

☐ Do you provide **conceptual images** (not simply illustrative) to help contextualize the lexical item?

☐ Does your item include a **spatial**, **sensory** or **motor** contextualization?

☐ Do you include **lexical chunks** and **collocations** to understand the different dimensions of the target structure?

☐ Are there **figurative uses** too? Are you developing your students' **metaphorical competence**?

☐ And how about **discursive uses** to understand the Cx in contextual cohesion? For example, are you using **mapped-out** texts?

☐ Do you favor **semantic relationships** between the lexical unit and other similar or related items? This can be done with mind maps, lexical categories, semantic fields...

☐ Do you include **morphological derivation** to help students go from nouns to verbs to adverbs, for instance? (that is, are you fostering **intralinguistic reflection** to make these connections?)

☐ Do you promote **interlinguistic reflection**? (i.e., discuss connections of the L2 with the L1 of your students so that they can understand the target form in a less foreign manner?)

☐ Have you considered **pedagogical translation**?

Figure 31 Cognitive lexis: a checklist for L2 instructors

Back in 2010, Boers, De Rycker, and De Knop expressed an idea that more than a decade later continues to be relevant and bears even more weight in light of the emergence of affordable and available technology for L2 education[34]:

> Ultimately, the future of any language theory lies in its relevance, i.e., the extent to which it addresses issues that are topical in the broader society, and its usefulness in terms of both the further development of the framework itself and the potential applications of the findings outside the academic world (p. 19).

Technology-based learning materials have enormous potential for the embodied and sensorimotor perspectives advocated by ACL, since they offer <u>animated</u>, <u>interactive,</u> and <u>digital</u> tools for effective content creation:

---

[34] It is important to note that very little research has been conducted with technology-based materials so far. Some promising examples include Arnett and Suñer 2019; Suñer and Roche 2021; Kissling & Arnold 2022; and Martín-Gascón et al. 2023, but more research is needed.

- **Animated** – via the use of GIFs (graphics interchange format) and other visual elements with integrated motion that can illustrate representational features of grammatical units, activate dynamic recognition of semantic features, or promote better retention of pragmatic, discursive, or collocational values. Grammatical topics in ACL such as aspect, for instance, can benefit from animated instruction, since the ongoing (unbounded) scope of the action can be represented with a GIF's repeated motion loop, signaling the open-ended verbal event. The terminated (bounded) action, on the other hand, can be elucidated by way of a short video that shows how a specific action has a beginning, a middle point and an ending, and that all three components are semantically embedded in the verbal ending of the tense. Arnett, Suñer & Pust (2019: 369) contribute additional support by adding that there is evidence that "dynamic forms of visualization are well suited to support cognitive linguistic grammar explanations, since they can represent the relevant dynamic aspects of grammar, force, movement, energy transfer, etc., more robustly than static pictures."
- **Interactive** – whereby students can "learn by doing," engaging with grammatical and lexical content in meaningful and collaborative ways. Figure 32[35] shows an interactive activity[36] created with the platform *Learningapps* for B1

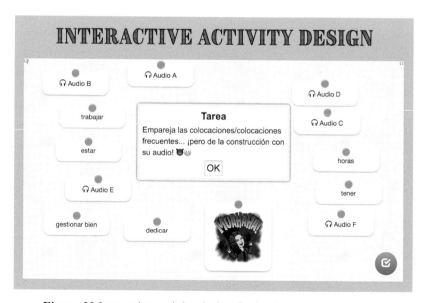

Figure 32 Interactive activity design for in-class or at-home work

[35] Prompt: Match the collocations and frequent collocation of the construction … with its audio component!

[36] https://learningapps.org/view20197084

Spanish. This is a collocational activity for vocabulary on the topic of TIME where students must listen to an audio prompt and match it with the word(s) that complete(s) the expression. Activities like these can be completed collaboratively in the classroom setting, which introduce an element of play and competition and foster connections between the aural and written patterns of the L2. Additionally, these kinds of self-assessing, interactive activities are especially important during asynchronous study, or the content from the textbook is not enough to "stimulate cognitive engagement" with the target language (Boers 2013: 213)

- **Digital** – so that content is available to use in class or at home. Digital materials are key for student engagement and meaningful practice beyond class time. *Flipped classroom* approaches, for instance, afford learners the option to interact with complex, difficult content in their own time and at their own pace, *before* coming to the more faster-paced classroom experience. As Román-Mendoza (2018: 31) points out, there is an important association "between the methodology of the flipped classroom in L2 and critical pedagogy, reflected in aspects such as accessibility, the use of time in class to learn meaningfully and not to teach, the autonomy of the learner and the scaffolding didactic." For the specific case of ACL materials, the flipped classroom philosophy gives learners time to access, consider, understand, and ultimately interact with the novel theoretical approaches and concepts that are so different from the teaching styles they may typically know (see Section 5). Figure 33 shows a slide[37] out of a 4:37 video for the difference between the Spanish verbs *ser* and *estar* (which in English translate to the single-verb option *to be*). Students in an A1-level course watched at home before coming to class to ask questions and then practice. The slide shows the spatial prototype of "outside the quality" as a circumstantial result of *force dynamics* for the verb *estar*. The text and images in the video have animations and the instructor's voice can be heard with the explanation of the prototype and its extended radial network. Because the video introduces a very new approach to the *ser/estar* contrast, it helps with processing if learners are able to watch at home, change the playback settings (faster or slower), and interact with the video at their own pace.

---

[37] Slide translation: With the verb ESTAR we express results. Circumstantial and resultative qualities. OUTSIDE. [In green headlines:] Circumstances that affect us/Now, not now/historical result. [And a list of examples in Spanish with the explanations of the radiality on "cause," "location," and "result."]

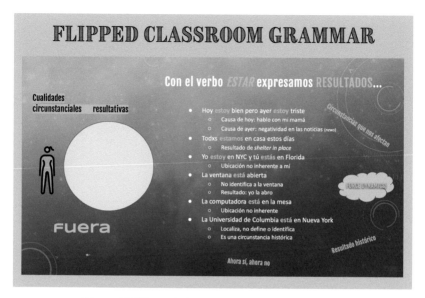

Figure 33 Flipped classroom material on grammar

4.2 Multimodality

One of the most relevant allies in ACL teaching materials is *multimodality*. From a CL perspective, this term refers to elements that occur alongside verbal language while also carrying semantic value. I am referring to co-speech gestures, bodily motions, facial expressions, and any other kinetic and visual channels that coexist with words in a communication event or that even substitute words altogether. Multimodality also refers to visual and auditory cues that substitute linguistic samples (such as an emoji, for instance) or more currently, the combination of image and text (i.e. memes, GIFs, or *Bitmoji*) to convey richer meanings and shared understandings at the social level (Dancygier & Vandelanotte 2017; Pérez-Sobrino 2017; Malinowski, Maxim, & Dubreil 2020; Forceville 2021).

Because memes and other visual contraptions typical of today's digital and social media-oriented communication are so prevalent and have become such an integrated part of linguistic exchanges between parties of all ages, their inclusion in teaching materials seems necessary and relevant: "These artifacts are well-known in a given discourse community and provide instant access to rich frames whose contribution to the emerging meaning is central" (Dancygier & Vandelanotte 2017: 568). Figure 34 shows B1-level, student-generated memes for form-focused practice of temporal clauses with the indicative and with periphrastic constructions, such

Figure 34 Multimodality and meme creation for meaning-making

as *seguir + gerund (continue to+infinitive)*, *dejar de + infinitive (stop+gerund)*. The activity allowed students to explore their own interpretation of contextual uses of grammatical constructions by using online meme generators. They then uploaded all memes to a *Padlet*[38] (i.e. a bulletin board-style tool that allows for collaborative multimedia and text postings) and shared with each other. Memes activate *Idealized Cognitive Models* (ICMs) (Kövecses 2002; Tay 2014), or categorized encyclopedic knowledge that allow speakers to partake in larger conceptual domains connected with cultural and contextual information. By triggering these ICMs, students practice active linguistic production and meaningful connections of form-and-semantics pairings.

Memes also have a very strong usage-based component, since the images are well-known and widely shared in social media and messaging apps in a plethora of contexts. In this case, it is the text that changes the interpretation of the image (which students in the exercise were capitalizing on).

Also, and as Torres and Aristu (2021) point out: "Advances in mobile technology have brought about a change in communications, both in form and content. The differences between oral and written communication have been blurred, tending towards communicative immediacy and multimodal registers" (p. 5–6). Multimodality combines text (aural or written), images, sounds, and embodied emotions (such as an emoji) in order to easily convey affective elements and moods "that breathe life and intensity into bare facts" (Castañeda Castro 2012: 257).

---

[38] https://padlet.com/RLLG/multimodalityandmemes

4.2.1 A Case Study: Mood Selection in Spanish

An example of what is meant by the above quote is provided in Figure 35, which depicts a slide from teaching materials on the indicative/subjunctive contrast (B1 level) and also an interactive activity[39] from *Learningapps*. Before going into the content of the material, what is worth remarking about this combination of a theoretical slide and a practice exercise is the coherence in the multimodal elements present. Suñer & Roche (2019: 5) recommend that "animations [and material design in general] must be designed in such a way that perceptually salient elements correspond with thematically and cognitively relevant elements for learning." Let us observe the material to illustrate the recommendation.

The top tier of the material has been designed with *Google Slides* and although it is part of a much larger presentation on the semantic prototypes of the indicative and the subjunctive in Spanish, there are certain elements to highlight. First, there are two distinct columns, left for the indicative and right for the subjunctive. Llopis-García (2009, 2011, 2019a) states that the prototype for mood selection is experiential and relates to IDENTIFICATION🔍: we identify information, facts, ideas, or moments in time and thus use the indicative. This

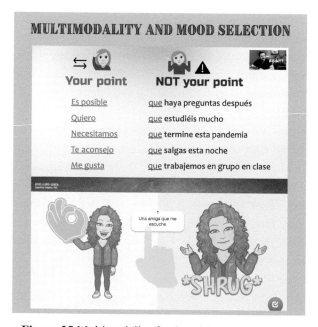

Figure 35 Multimodality for Spanish mood selection

---

[39] https://learningapps.org/view20254569

identification (ID🔍) becomes *one's point* (like the left column indicates) and the double arrow conveys that if both clauses (main and subordinate) have an identification🔍, they come to represent the same idea. The emoji of the woman speaker conveys assurance: her features are positive, she smiles, and the raised hand indicates confidence in the statement: she identifies what she says. The green color, which represents completion (like the "done"✅ emoji) or the ability to move forward (like a traffic light 🚥) also embodies the attitude of the indicative.

If, however, the communicative intent of the speaker is to NOT identify a communicative event but to still want to say something about it, the use of the subjunctive is required: it represents a non-identification (non-ID🤷) of what is said and allows the speakers to convey a personal assertion, a value judgment, a denial, a justification, a comment … without it *being the focal point* of the intent. The non-ID🤷 of the subjunctive is, as the examples above show, the verb of the subordinate clause. In the words of Llopis-García (2019a: 262. OT): "in the sentences that select the subjunctive in its subordination, processing gives priority to the verb of the main clause, while relegating … the subordinate verb as background, thus creating an asymmetry between the communicative value of both processes." In the emoji of the non-ID, the woman speaker has a gesture of non-committal attitude: a shrug 🤷, meaning that what is being said cannot be identified as a main/focal point. There can be any positive or negative outtakes on what is being said, but that information is *not conveyed* by the subjunctive itself, and the triangle with the exclamation point (⚠) references this. The color for the *not your point* that relates to the non-ID🤷 is purple and the relationship between the main clause (an ID🔍) and the subordinate clause (a non-ID🤷) cannot be equated.

As an additional affective tweak for an embodied and cultural notion, there is a GIF on the upper right corner that brings popular American TV culture to the understanding of the subjunctive in Spanish: the beloved deadpan and sarcastic character of Ron Swanson (performed by actor Nick Offerman) in the TV show *Parks and Recreation* (2009–2015). On the GIF, his questioning gestures, together with the text (*What's your point?*) represent the attitude conveyed by the non-ID🤷 of the subjunctive, adding an extra layer of embodied interpretation to the abstract meaning of the linguistic form.

The lower tier of Figure 35 includes an interactive activity[40] for the first extended use of the semantic extension (or *radial network*) of mood selection, which moves from the general prototype of ID/non-ID to the specific case of relative clauses (see Llopis-García 2009 for a further elaboration of

---

[40] https://learningapps.org/view20254569

the radial network). For clauses of description, "students learn that entities can be described in two ways: by identifying them and noting that something specific, known and visualized is being described, ... or on the contrary, by describing them as something unknown, not recognized and therefore not identified" (Llopis-García 2019a: 263. OT). The prompt for the activity (not included in the image) is "organize the following sentences depending on whether they are IDENTIFIED (🙋) or NON-IDENTIFIED (🤷) ideas/objects/people." It is worth noticing that the *Bitmoji* that represent the prototypes are consistent with the emoji from the theoretical slides and from the prompt. Additionally, the indicative from the main clauses is located on the left side of the screen (like on the slide), whereas the subjunctive, which can be found exclusively in the subordinate clause, is on the right side of the screen. The color coordination is also notable, since the ID🙋 Bitmoji has a raised hand and a green glove, and the non-ID Bitmoji🤷 is blue (a closer color to purple) and is shrugging to represent the noncommittal attitude of the subjunctive. The activity includes a total of ten identical examples that differ *only* in the subordinate verb. Students must then focus on this verb to solve the exercise (see Section 3.1.2). The sentence depicted in the image is *A friend who **listens** to me*, where the verb *listens* can be construed with the indicative or the subjunctive. As students encounter either sentence, their focus will be on whether they know who the friend is (an ID🙋 and hence an indicative: *escucha*) or whether they don't know/can't decide who that friend might be (a non-ID🤷 and hence a subjunctive: *escuche*).

From the analysis of this material, it stands that the *perceptual saliency* of the prototype of mood is coherent with the thematic aspects of its description, as suggested by the earlier quote by Suñer and Roche (2019). The multimodal elements in this pedagogical material bring together embodied, constructional, and representational features of a linguistic topic of great relevance and high difficulty for both instructors and students. They "are best suited for presenting linguistic and sensorimotor aspects in an integrated way, allowing for more accurate mental representations of the grammatical concepts" (Suñer & Roche, 2019: 10).

4.2.2 Multimodal Tools for Technology-Based Learning

The use of multimodal elements provides opportunities to turn linguistic knowledge into visual, relatable, and accessible content. Back in Section 2.3 about metaphorical competence, the need for visual aids to help learners make sense of the linguistic structure of the L2 was called into relevance because it affects conceptual understanding during the L2 learning process (Boers 2011, 2013; Castañeda Castro 2012, 2014; Llopis-García 2015, 2016b, 2021a, 2021b; Suñer & Roche 2019; Arnett & Suñer 2019). Multimodal elements:

- **Integrate** form, meaning, speaker stance, or communicative intent in a way that language alone would not be able to convey to the full extent of its semantic potential. They facilitate understanding as if linguistic constructions were objects that we can "see," as in Figure 8 with the embodied phonological and morphological connotations of *dizzy/mareado*, or the radial network of the preposition *hasta/up to* in Figure 14. Additionally, as seen with the aspectual difference between the imperfect and the preterit in Spanish (Figures 16–18), a right-or-wrong approach to understanding proves challenging, since there are very few cases in which using either yields an agrammatical use. Multimodality helps navigate formal differences and empowers learners to choose based on *communicative intent* and not on taxonomies brought on by the textbook.

- Can help learners **distinguish** between linguistic forms that otherwise would make them rely solely on memorization and drill practice for uptake into procedural knowledge. Consider the topic of quantification, typically taught at the A1 level and where learners often have lists of examples to work through for countable and uncountable nouns (see Figure 36), but also for adjectives and verbs. For these forms, the combinations are slightly similar but not the same, making the differentiation between all categories a true challenge. Teaching materials can provide self-explanatory images

Figure 36 Image use for embodied and representational grammar

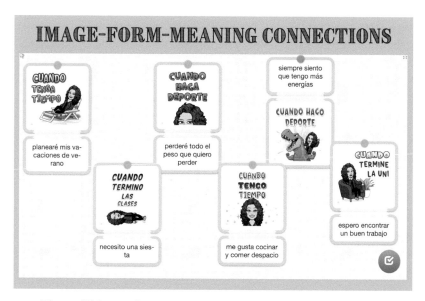

Figure 37 Image-form-meaning connection via interactive activity

that embody and represent what each quantifying category represents by keeping the examples coherent by topic. Boers (2013: 219) points out that "instead of steering learners towards a more holistic mode of processing multiword lexis, CL pedagogy actually intends to harness learners' analytic abilities"

- Show how complex grammatical Cxs are represented by images to not only **clarify and help** with the understanding of semantic differences, but also to provide "the context of the dynamic discourse" in which they happen (Castañeda Castro 2012: 260). Figure 37 shows the finalized result of an interactive activity[41] with Learningapps for mood at the B1 level. Through the contextualized use of *Bitmoji* and the visual elements represented in both image and text, students can better determine if the temporal clause (with *cuando/when*) represents the ID👍😀 of a familiar moment or the non-ID😬😀 of a future event to come. Alhmoud, Castañeda Castro, and Cadierno (2019: 217) support the meaningful use of images, multimodal cues, and text because they become self-explanatory (versus the merely informative image we so often find in textbooks). They also add dynamism and clarity to the linguistic structure at hand.

The digital market of applications and platforms for educational technology is ever-growing and there are new ideas and projects being released to language

---

[41] https://learningapps.org/view20254703

instructors, content creators, material developers, and research designers alike all the time. However, the choices are many and their selection will depend on a variety of personal preferences: clarity of purpose, user-friendly operation, teaching and learning objectives, lesson planning and time availability, user's digital competence, or student's ability to operate and interact with the material. It is therefore up to every professional to find their "digital entourage" in order to explore a multimedia and multimodal approach to ACL teaching and learning.

4.3 Final Considerations

Section 4 has taken a deeper dive into material creation driven by principles and guidelines from CL. It has also provided real classroom examples to demonstrate the *how to* of ACL design and has explained the rationale behind the choices in educational technology and in the grammatical explanations driving activity design. It is my hope that the examples here (with an ongoing invitation for the reader to use and adapt) may inspire a clearer path to teaching content that is attractive, coherent, engaging, interactive, and memorable for L2 learners.

5 Cognitive Empirical Design

5.1 The Importance of Professional Development for L2 Instructors

Throughout this Element, foundational constructs from CL have been applied to the teaching of the grammar and lexis continuum at all levels of competence. This has been done from the perspective and experience of linguists who are language instructors (like me), and of language instructors with a professional development and background in linguistics.

A survey conducted with 71 instructors of Spanish/L2 after taking professional development on CL and L2 instruction[42] shows interesting results. When asked the question *Do you think cognitive approaches are useful in the Spanish classroom (in general)?*, 93 percent of instructors (66 participants) gave the question a 3 and the remaining 7 percent (five participants) chose to stay in the

---

[42] This survey was conducted in 2020 and 2021 with instructors who took one out of two professional development courses at an introductory level that I teach on CL and L2. The responses were anonymous and were recorded on a voluntary basis after completion of the courses, which were online and in asynchronous form via videos, forum discussions, and collaborative Padlet boards. One of the courses had a duration of two weeks and the other, an extended version of the first, of four weeks. The answers were measured on a Likert scale of 1–3, 1 being the lowest assessment, 2 a middle option, and 3 the highest. Every question gave participants the chance to elaborate on their answer and explain further.

middle. No one selected 1. From those who chose to voluntarily elaborate on their answers, some opinions were:

- "I believe that one of the main contributions is **giving learners the leading role** ... (one that is traditionally given to the instructor or the textbooks). It seems fundamental to give students the power to be creators of meanings and imitators of patterns." (OT) Gibbs (2020), addressing MacArthur's work on metaphorical competence and student creativity in L2, agrees with this statement, arguing that "novel or hybrid metaphors enable second language learners from different cultural and linguistic backgrounds to effectively communicate in ways that simply parroting conventional metaphor may be unable to do" (p. 30)
- "It is much easier for students to learn **something that seems logical to them**, than what must be learned because they have been told that it is so, and that's the end to it." (OT) This opinion is in line with Littlemore & Juchen-Grundman (2010): "Discussing the reasons why certain words are used in certain situations has the potential to remove the arbitrariness from language teaching and is potentially more effective than a reliance on rote memorisation, or simply being told by a teacher that 'that's just the way it is'" (p. 7)
- "Before the course I had many unnamed concepts in my pedagogical repertoire, now I have learned to consciously specify many techniques that I have been putting into practice through activities in my classes, in all cases with **excellent feedback** from my students." (OT) Holme (2010b), after working with a high school class on an experiment about Cxs, and even though he was warned of the students' reluctance to engage, found that, as his study progressed, "the class were generally willing to participate in an exercise and showed trust in the benefits of the procedures used" (p. 372) (Also see Kissling et al. 2018: 249, for more positive feedback from students.)
- "They **give instructors more confidence** in their explanations because of rigorous reflection and internalization of the symbiosis between form and meaning. ... **'Being hit' with the list of exceptions** (which almost always exist) causes the teacher's explanations to be judged and questioned." (OT) "They help to better situate ourselves in the communicative context and to approach the language as a whole, **overcoming the 'lists.'**" (OT) For these last two opinions, Llopis-García (2009) offers support for ACL instructor training because "understanding the grammar of an L2 from this point of view means freeing oneself from the lists of rules that assign forms to some meanings and the same meanings to different forms" (p. 96. OT).

Throughout these sample answers, two interesting opinion patterns emerge, one about ACL impact on students and the other about the impact on instructors themselves. For the former, instructors highlight the ability to empower students to learn from representational logic and to trust their communicative intent. The latter is also about empowerment, but this time for those who teach, because lists of rules and exceptions, so common in textbooks, disenfranchise instructors from owning insights into the languages they teach. CL can, at the very least, open new possibilities for instructors on the representational understanding of the L2.

Even though this survey by no means claims to be representative of the L2 teaching population, it does show that professional development is of interest and is deemed valuable by instructors. The availability of training in methodological developments in the L2 classroom is paramount if the ACL approach is to make it into "the mainstream" and become a familiar staple in the class. This, in turn, can result in teaching materials that include ACL and, eventually, cause more textbooks and guidelines to feature them as well. Training language instructors to "see things" from a cognitive perspective will benefit their pedagogical practice and the learning of their students. But also, and this is of the utmost importance, it will help linguists and researchers carry out more successful empirical classroom-based studies. Section 5.2 will explain why.

5.2 Empirical Research in ACL

The last two decades have seen the rise of CL in its intersection with L2 language pedagogy, and the very first empirical studies date back to the 1990s (Danesi 1992, 1993; Deignan et al. 1997; Boers 2011). Since then, the ever-growing body of research is a testament to the interest in and the potential of this intersection. Many references have already been documented in the prior pages and yet they amount to a small (albeit important) sample of what is being contributed to the field.

However, although these are all signs of a healthy discipline, there is one reason for concern: most empirical studies comparing cognitive approaches with more traditional methodologies for the teaching of grammar and lexis yield only partial (or no) superiority of the cognitive group versus the traditional one.[43] Suñer and Roche (2019: 4) point out that "studies . . . fail to document an

---

[43] For a list of specific studies that fail to show this superiority, the reading of Suñer and Roche (2019) and Arnett and Suñer (2019) is recommended. Lam (2009), Kissling et al. (2018), as well as two unpublished studies by Llopis-García & Alonso-Aparicio (conducted in 2017 and 2018) can be added to those mentioned in the two suggested references. However, the list increases if

overall positive effect on language learning compared with traditional form-based approaches."

The compendium of only partially successful or inconclusive studies, however, reveals a common issue in all of them. Arnett and Suñer (2019) come very close to the matter because these studies "neglect to look into features that could have affected the success of a cognitive linguistic approach such as the mode of presentation (e.g. multimedia animations) or integration into a task-based setting" (p. 366). After a thorough literature review, the authors recommend that "in the future, empirical research should be expanded to include **different task types and testing techniques** in order to provide a deeper analysis of the effects of cognitive linguistic approaches on the learning process" (p. 370).

This is the common thread: all reviewed studies feature assessment design that is crafted in line with the other teaching approach, NOT the cognitive one. Typical assessment tasks include grammaticality judgments, fill-in-the-blank exercises, multiple choice questions, or true/false statements **within the correct/incorrect dichotomy**. Kissling et al. (2018: 243), in a study on the contrast of the prepositions *por/para* in Spanish, reported that "fill-in-the-blank tests are commonly used for assessment of *por* and *para* and so allow for some comparison between our findings and those of other language programs and researchers." This statement is very important, as it offers one of the possible reasons for the status quo of assessment task design: previous studies use these types of tasks, so it follows that subsequent ones must as well. But it can also be argued: Why is research assessing learning gains from a new methodology with **tasks that *do not resemble*** what participants have just learned?

Llopis-García & Alonso-Aparicio (2018, 2019) and Llopis-García (2021b) have called attention to this issue, arguing that correct-versus-incorrect instruction is what students *know*. Testing that reinforces previous learning experiences is counterproductive for the cognitive groups, who receive never-before-seen instruction. In the exam-based culture of most L2 instructional settings, students *know* how to take tests with multiple choices and blanks to fill because they have been part of their daily routine (outside of empirical studies) for a long time. And although assessment in L2 has long been a difficult topic of contention that is outside the scope of this Element, the main concern in this case is that **traditional tasks can measure linguistic *accuracy* and knowledge of rules, but not necessarily linguistic *understanding* of the target items** (which is what ACL promotes). More to the point: multiple choice or fill-in-the-blank tests check for correct understanding/use of the rules learned during the instruction, but they do not measure *whether or how*

---

we also take into account inconclusive studies presented at CL conferences that never see the light of publishing.

learners apprehended the inner workings of the linguistic form at hand. Assessment task design continues to prioritize the selection of linguistic forms (i.e. imperfect/ preterit) without really being able to measure if the students truly know the difference. Martín-Gascón et al. (2023) add to this belief by stating that:

> ACL methods … focus on embodiment, semantic motivation, image-based form and meaning pairings, or the saliency of communicative intent. These pedagogical notions veer greatly from the more automated answer choices of traditional tasks, so assessing the effects of a novel, brand new instruction with traditional methods stacks the odds against the cognitive groups every time.

There is also an issue of optics at play in the majority of studies reported in the literature review of the field. Results fail to show a superiority of the cognitive approach over the traditional one because the comparison usually yields no statistically significant results between instruction groups. The discussion sections, then, argue different reasons for why this has happened. A small but representative sample includes causes such as (a) the approach was too new or complex for the students (Lam 2009; Bielak & Pawlak 2011; Arnett & Suñer 2019); (b) the sequence of presentation of instructional materials may have had an effect (Kissling et al. 2018); (c) assigned homework may have given students extra time to interact with the target form (Alonso-Aparicio & Llopis-García 2019); and (d) the closest reason to the issue at hand: "the nearly equal short-term gains for the two groups suggest that the control group [i.e. traditional] used the strategies they were accustomed to and had already mastered" (Zhao et al. 2018: 275). It is from this last statement that the heart of the matter emerges.

In all studies that showed no statistical differences between the cognitive and other-instruction groups – when the assessment had used correct-versus-incorrect tasks – the issue is not that the cognitive *could not* outperform the more traditional group. Rather, *the great accomplishment* is that the cognitive group, even though they received a completely new instruction, still managed to perform *as well as* the other group. Despite the absence of methodological coherence in the assessment of a novel instruction type, the cognitive group still achieved the same – or higher – learning gains as their counterpart, who received 'familiar instruction + familiar tests.'

If ACL is based on the representational semantics of linguistic forms, how can a fill-in-the-blank activity[44] check for the understanding of semantic motivation? The stance here is that novel instruction that moves beyond a *"use the correct form"* prompt requires novel data collection design. The questions to ask, then:

---

[44] It actually can, but if stated/reformulated to fit an ACL-based type of question. See Figures 40, 41a, and 41b for the alternatives.

(1) What would happen if learning gains were measured with task design consistent with the methodology of cognitive instruction?
(2) What if this new design also took more traditional elements (such as metalanguage) into account?
(3) Would the cognitive group show a statistically significant advantage over the other instruction methodology in production and interpretation tasks?

These questions can be addressed with results from a pilot and a main study that may open new avenues for research and represent a departure from previous studies.

5.2.1 Alternative Empirical Design: A Study

In order to address the issues with assessment task design, a pilot and a main study[45] (six months apart) were conducted to evaluate the viability of the proposals addressed in the prior section. The entirety of the research happened online, since all teaching was being conducted in that manner since the beginning of the COVID-19 pandemic in March 2020, and all conditions from the pilot study were kept constant during the replication. The duration was of three, 75-minute class sessions spanning a week and a half and participants completed a pretest, received instruction plus an immediate posttest two days after, and then a delayed posttest four days after. The method of delivery was online via Zoom for instruction and the tests took 20 minutes each and were completed via Wufoo, an online platform for testing. Assessment tasks included interpretation and production of the target form, which was the psych-verb construction for the expression of emotion with the verbs *gustar/to like, encantar/to love, interesar/to be interested in, molestar/to bother,* and *fastidiar/to annoy.* Consistent with what has been suggested throughout this Element about the importance of introducing ACL from the start of the learning process, the study was carried out at the A1/elementary level with N= 40 students in the pilot study (from an initial pool of 52), and with N= 140 in the main study (from an initial pool of 160). Students were distributed into three conditions: two instruction groups, cognitive linguistics group (CLG) and traditional[46] group (TG), plus

---

[45] I will not address the study in full detail here because of space constraints. The study, its statistical data, and its results are in Martín-Gascón, Llopis-García and Alonso-Aparicio 2023.

[46] By traditional instruction, we mean here a notional-functional approach, modeled after many textbooks in the market. This instruction offers grammatical metalanguage and tables that organize grammar and activities for comprehension and production that are based on correct-versus-incorrect answers. This is also consistent with what other empirical studies mentioned have implemented, and not with what classroom-based teaching methodologies might be doing on a daily basis.

a control group (CG), who did not receive any instruction but completed all assessment tests.[47]

The pilot study grouped participants in intact course sections, resulting in CLG = 18, TG = 16, and CG = 6. The main study followed the same procedure and was sorted into CLG = 59, TG = 49, and CG = 32. Learners were in their first semester of Spanish at a North American university and those who made it into the study scored below 60 percent on the pretest and attended all sessions.

The research questions, alongside a positive answer for the hypotheses, were:

(1) What is the relative effect of an ACL-inspired approach and a traditional approach to teaching psych-verbs when learning gains are measured with ACL-inspired assessment interpretation tasks?

(2) What is the relative effect of an ACL-inspired approach and a traditional approach to teaching psych-verbs when learning gains are measured with ACL-inspired assessment production tasks?

The instructional materials for the traditional group were inspired by many market-ready textbooks, with a presentation of the target structure and practice activities. There was a text flooded with highlighted target forms for discussion and inductive understanding (Figure 38a). The structure of the psych-verb construction was presented with tables, like it is common in textbooks (Figure 38b), but the slides also contained the metalanguage from the cognitive instruction (i.e. *experiencer, stimulus/idea*) to ensure fairness in the assessment tasks. Active practice exercises in interpretation and production of the Cx followed and students worked individually and in groups.

The instructional materials for the cognitive group focused on the comparison of "normal verbs" (i.e. those with a subject-verb-object structure) versus "verbs of emotion" and used GIFs and moving arrows to represent the object-verb-subject structure of the Cx (Figure 39a on page 80). The instruction included ACL concepts such as *embodiment, perspective,* or *motivation* of the Cx, while at the same time adding the more frequent metalanguage of the other group as well (Figure 39b). Just as with the TG, all participants practiced the interpretation and production of target structures after instruction, both individually and with other students.

---

[47] It is important to note that this study, because of the pool of participants, the learning context, or the duration of the study, has limited generalizability. It constitutes, however, an alternative for task design and a novel approach that we hope will inspire other studies or offer new ideas for research.

(a)

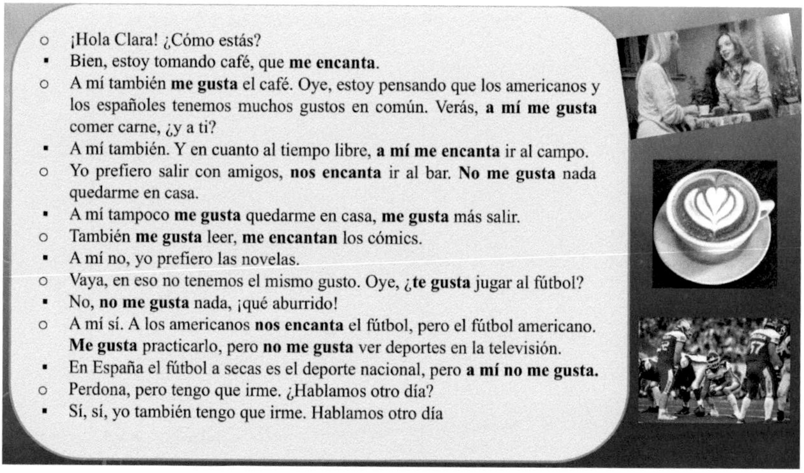

o ¡Hola Clara! ¿Cómo estás?
• Bien, estoy tomando café, que **me encanta**.
o A mí también **me gusta** el café. Oye, estoy pensando que los americanos y los españoles tenemos muchos gustos en común. Verás, **a mí me gusta** comer carne, ¿y a ti?
• A mí también. Y en cuanto al tiempo libre, **a mí me encanta** ir al campo.
o Yo prefiero salir con amigos, **nos encanta** ir al bar. **No me gusta** nada quedarme en casa.
• A mí tampoco **me gusta** quedarme en casa, **me gusta** más salir.
o También **me gusta** leer, **me encantan** los cómics.
• A mí no, yo prefiero las novelas.
o Vaya, en eso no tenemos el mismo gusto. Oye, ¿**te gusta** jugar al fútbol?
• No, **no me gusta** nada, ¡qué aburrido!
o A mí sí. A los americanos **nos encanta** el fútbol, pero el fútbol americano. **Me gusta** practicarlo, pero **no me gusta** ver deportes en la televisión.
• En España el fútbol a secas es el deporte nacional, pero **a mí no me gusta**.
o Perdona, pero tengo que irme. ¿Hablamos otro día?
• Sí, sí, yo también tengo que irme. Hablamos otro día

(b)

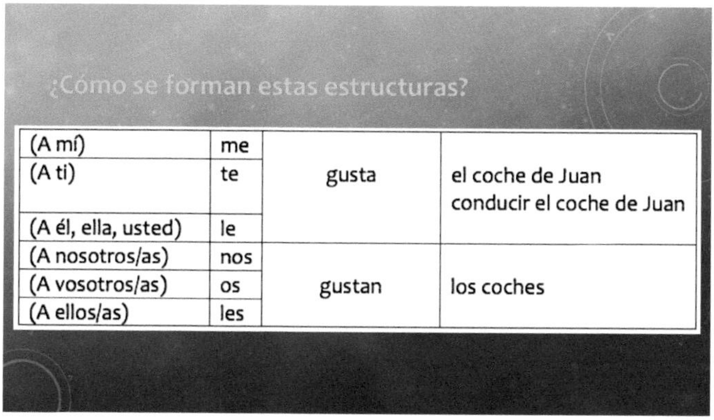

¿Cómo se forman estas estructuras?

(A mí)	me		
(A ti)	te	gusta	el coche de Juan
			conducir el coche de Juan
(A él, ella, usted)	le		
(A nosotros/as)	nos		
(A vosotros/as)	os	gustan	los coches
(A ellos/as)	les		

Figure 38a Traditional instruction I,
and b Traditional instruction II

Assessment Task Design

As explained before, all participating students completed a pretest and two posttests (immediately after the instruction and four days after). Each test took 20 minutes, and it had interpretation and production tasks. In line with Lam (2009), who included an option on her tests for the students to explain how certain they were of their answer, our participants were strongly advised *not to guess*, to answer only if they were certain, and to use the additional option of *Skip it!* any time they were unsure of an answer. They were assured that all testing would not impact their grades.

The **interpretation tasks** (Figure 40 and also Figure 23 in earlier pages) asked students to match images to linguistic forms for meaning understanding,

(a)

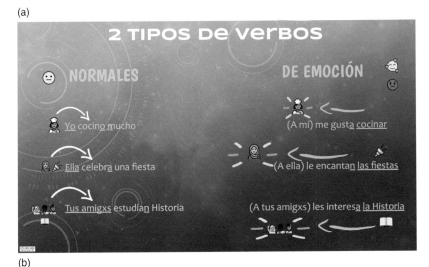

(b)

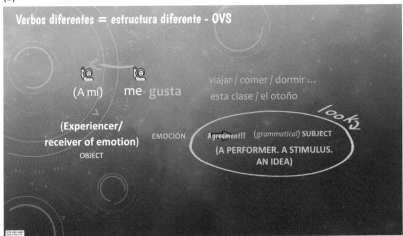

Figure 39a Cognitive instruction I,
and b Cognitive instruction II

used motivated concepts such as *experiencer, performer, stimulus,* or *main idea*, as well as the traditional counterparts of *indirect object* or *subject* for balanced access of both instructional groups. Notice how the FonF activity can only be completed if the role of each participant in the construction is understood. Language becomes representational and meaning becomes grammatical. Visual representation stands for a show of understanding because there is less focus on metalanguage, and the words *correct/incorrect*, in line with traditional testing types, are never used.

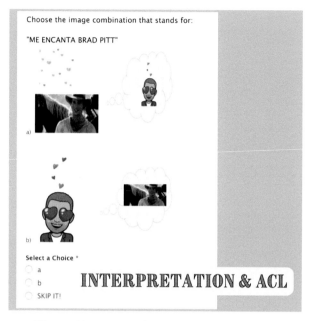

Figure 40 Interpretation task with ACL design

The production tasks (however basic, since students were beginners) were also meaning-based and asked participants to explicitly identify the *experiencer*, the verb of emotion, or the *stimulus/idea*, and even though these were ACL terms, they had also been featured in the traditional instruction package and in the other activities. The focus of these tasks was on "who's who" in the psychverb Cx in order to show understanding of the structure (Figure 41a, following on from Figure 40, and Figure 41b).

The assessment tests followed an ACL design that incorporated focus on form techniques. They made students focus on the motivated, embodied, and representational features of the psych-verb Cx, so understanding of the semantic roles of subjects (main ideas/stimuli/performers) and objects (experiencers) was a *sine qua non* condition to complete the exercise. The fact that the terminology used addressed both cognitive and traditional content ensured that neither instructional group was at a disadvantage with respect to the other. As most empirical studies conducted to date show, this has historically not been the case, since assessment tasks did not include the newly learned terminology or format of the cognitive instruction.

(a)

(b)

Figure 41a Production task with ACL design I,
and b Production task with ACL design II

Results[48]

Figures 42 and 43 show that, in both the pilot and the main study, the CLG was statistically superior to both the TG and the CG. This difference applied to posttest analysis, since at the pretest all groups tested the same. The superiority of learning gains applied to both the interpretation and the production tasks, and

---

[48] Again, for full data, analysis and details, see Martín-Gascón, Llopis-García and Alonso Aparicio 2023.

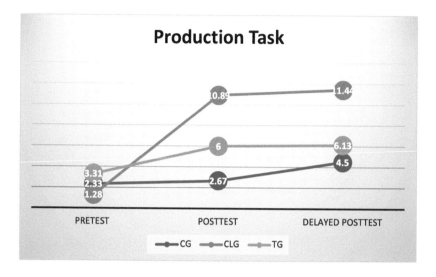

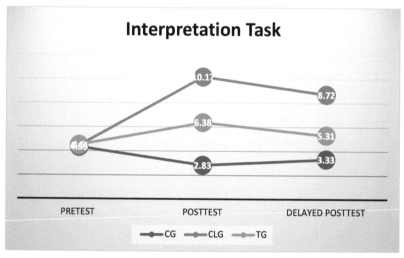

Figure 42 PILOT study results

while both instructional groups made learning gains (statistically superior to those of the CG), it was the CG that took the lead in both.

It is worth mentioning that the TG "did show improved performance in both tasks and both tests after the intervention, yet the improvement in their learning outcomes was not superior to the CLG, even when the assessment also included the terminology that they had been exposed to during their instruction session." (Martín-Gascón et al., 2023) This further offers support to the point that more inclusive assessment design yields positive results in both instructional groups, although more so for our target methodology.

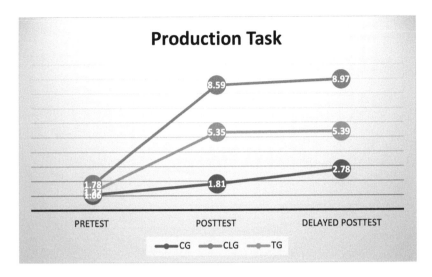

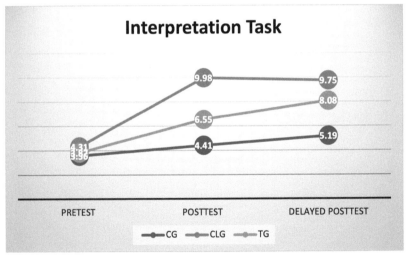

Figure 43 MAIN study results

Conclusions: New Avenues Open Up

To our knowledge, these two studies are the first of their kind because they used ACL principles to design the **assessment tasks**, and not rule-based, more notional-functional practice (such as correct-versus-incorrect grammaticality judgments or fill-in-the-blanks). It also included metalanguage accessible to both instructional groups in the assessment.

The results confirm that both instructional groups made learning gains. However, as our research hypotheses had predicted and in line with claims by

Llopis-García and Alonso-Aparicio (2018, 2019) and Llopis-García (2021b), the lead came from the CLG, and this opens up new pathways of research moving forward. Because ACL offers relatable and accessible explanations based on the understanding of sensorimotor experiences, the students from the TG were also able to complete the assessment tasks. And finally, the CLG was able to surpass the traditional one in both types of tasks because the assessment was in line with the instruction they had received.

Even though L2 methodologies have evolved enormously *in the classroom*, empirical research has continued to operate with the abstract and largely undefined term of traditional instruction (TI), meaning any kind of notional-functional, right-versus-wrong approach. Therefore, the methodological status quo has not changed because empirical research has continued to apply TI to the design of assessment, unfairly, and always giving the so-called traditional group an advantage over the target methodology of the study.

What the study in this section shows is that a cognitive-based instruction can be compatible with these notional-functional approaches to the teaching of grammar and lexis, thus contributing to covering more diverse learning styles and maximizing the learning experience of the students. What is more important: results empirically validate the claims of ACL which are currently only partially supported by both research and anecdotal evidence (i.e. teachers' reflections on their classroom practice).

5.3 Final Considerations

The beginning of this section showed results from a voluntary survey with instructors of Spanish/L2 and emphasized the need for professional development. ACL-trained instructors can make a difference in their classrooms AND they can also bring ACL approaches to the forefront of methodological action and turn them into mainstream, accessible content for other instructors and also textbook publishers. What is more: new and promising collaborations could emerge between linguists/researchers, publishers, and language instructors. Suñer and Roche 2019, Holme 2010a, and Alonso-Aparicio and Llopis-García 2019 (among others) have defended the need for these collaborations in order to adapt abstract schemas to the L2 classroom for pedagogical maximization. Figure 44 shows the transition from CL concepts to ACL classroom material, which then translated into what was shown earlier in Figures 16a to 18.

Mutual feedback between instructors and researchers can contribute to solving the issue of empirical shortcomings. On the one hand, the presence of researchers in the L2 classroom is often limited to the day of their experiment, and their lack of teaching experience can impact material design and/or how

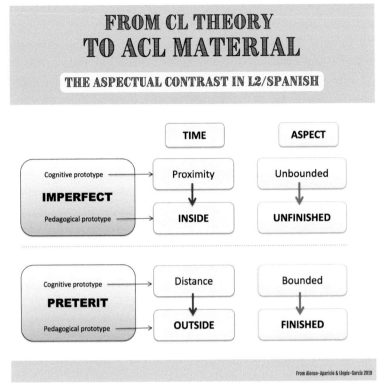

Figure 44 From CL theory to ACL material

students receive it. On the other hand, course instructors are the professionals of content creation and are in tune with learning objectives and the students in their class. Surely this cooperation makes sense. Researchers could benefit immensely from instructor input on their material design, and ACL-trained instructors could also enrich their grasp on the newly learned constructs and concepts from collaborating with researchers. This, in turn, would enrich daily L2 teaching that could normalize the presence of ACL in the classroom and foster the much-sought student familiarity with the methodology for easier, more effective implementation of research studies.

6 Conclusions

The aim of this Element was not to advocate for incorporating ACL into L2 pedagogy, since that call has been well documented in the literature since the early 2000s. The purpose here, instead, has been to show what the merging of L2 + ACL *already* looks like. There is pedagogical content of value being developed and used, and the L2 community is now aware of it *and interested* in it. Finally, there is research being actively conducted in the right direction.

The pedagogical adaptations of CL constructs and foundational ideas presented here are the fruits of long-term classroom experience and of collaborative work with colleagues in the field of L2 pedagogy, as well as with fellow linguists and researchers. This Element showcases the cooperation between disciplines and aims to be an example of what this continued alliance could bring for all intended audiences.

Throughout these pages, I have offered insights into how ACL matters for quality teaching and learning, with content offering systemic and motivated explanations of grammatical and lexical constructions. From an L2 instruction perspective, language is not a phenomenon to observe and document, and it should not be learned in isolation from usage. An ACL-based approach aims at dispensing with the perceived "foreignness" of another language, seeking access to the conceptualization process of the language and culture without forgetting one's own L1. A general summary of ideas from ACL teaching include:

- The motivation of meaning for experiential awareness and fostered memorability of grammar and lexis in the L2. The experiential basis and the study of *perspective* make concepts in the L2 more accessible and relatable, thus decreasing the need for blind memorization
- The development of the metaphorical competence of learners to normalize inter- and intralinguistic reasoning and create connections between the languages they know. This starts with their L1s, moves on to their L3s and continues with the interlanguage of the L2
- The use of prototypes to inform morphosyntactic and semantic information within linguistic units, and of constructions to highlight how these relationships are systematic and can lead to more fluency and a better grasp of the system
- Educational technology is a strong ACL ally to represent all of the above, and SLA insights into current L2 learning methodologies also show compatibility with ACL teaching styles.

On the topic of research, Section 5 has brought the biggest issue related to empirical studies to the forefront: the majority of data cannot confirm the superiority of a cognitive methodology over a notional-functional approach. I have argued that the issue lies with assessment task design for the elicitation of data, which includes correct-versus-incorrect, rule-management activities that favor and are coherent with the latter approaches. Cognitive groups (CLGs), who receive brand-new instruction, face impossible odds when the assessment of their learning looks nothing like what they have just learned. From the pages of this Element, a call for different assessment design is followed by empirical evidence that this change may yield learning gains that favor the CLG. And although much more research is needed, a first step for a different design is offered here.

Once it can be empirically proven that ACL can be superior to more traditional methodologies when the assessment design is coherent with the teaching, if researchers and instructors joined forces in both study design and implementation, the field could make colossal advances in the years to come. And then everybody wins, especially, and above all, L2 learners.

References

Achard, M. (2008) "Teaching construal: Cognitive pedagogical grammar," in Robinson, P. and Ellis, N.C. (eds.) *Handbook of Cognitive Linguistics and Second Language Learning*. New York: Routledge, pp. 442–465.

Achard, M. (2018) "Teaching usage and concepts: Toward a cognitive pedagogical grammar," in A. Tyler, L. Huang, and H. Jan (eds.) *What is Applied Cognitive Linguistics?* Berlin: De Gruyter, pp. 37–62. https://doi.org/10.1515/9783110572186-002.

Achard, M. and Niemeier, S. (eds.) (2004) *Cognitive Linguistics, Second Language Acquisition, and Foreign Language Teaching.* . Berlin: Mouton de Gruyter (Studies on Language Acquisition). https://doi.org/10.1515/9783110199857.

Acquaroni, R. (2008) "La incorporación de la competencia metafórica (CM) a la enseñanza-aprendizaje del español como segunda lengua (L2) a través de un taller de escritura creativa. Estudio experimental." Unpublished dissertation. Universidad Complutense de Madrid. http://site.ebrary.com/id/10505443 (Accessed: March 1, 2022).

Acquaroni Muñoz and Suárez-Campos, L. (2019). 'El desarrollo de la competencia metafórica en la enseñanza del español LE/L2', In Ibarretxe-Antuñano, I., Cadierno, T., & Castañeda Castro, A. (eds.) *Lingüística cognitiva y español LE/L2*. New York: Routledge. 371–390

Aguiló-Mora, F. and Negueruela-Azarola, E. (2015) "Motion for the other through motion for the self: The conceptual complexities of giving-directions for advanced Spanish heritage learners," in K. Masuda, C. Arnett, and A. Labarca (eds.) *Cognitive Linguistics and Sociocultural Theory*. Berlin: De Gruyter, pp. 73–100. https://doi.org/10.1515/9781614514442-006.

Alejaldre-Biel, L. (2018) "Movilizar la enseñanza de ELE para aumentar la participación espontánea: estudio de caso con alumnos universitarios tailandeses," *El Guiniguada. Revista de investigaciones y experiencias en Ciencias de la Educación*, pp. 55–70. https://doi.org/10.20420/ElGuiniguada.2018.206.

Alejo-González, R. (2010) "Making sense of phrasal verbs: A cognitive linguistic account of L2 learning," *AILA Review*, 23, pp. 50–71. https://doi.org/10.1075/aila.23.04ale.

Alhmoud, Z., Castañeda Castro, A., and Cadierno, T. (2019) "Construcciones comparativas. Aproximación descriptiva y didáctica desde la gramática cognitiva," in I. Ibarretxe-Antuñano, T. Cadierno, and A. C. Castro (eds.) *Lingüística cognitiva y español LE/L2*. Oxford: Routledge, pp. 189–219.

Alonso-Aparicio, I. (2014) "Fundamentos cognitivos de la práctica sistemática en la enseñanza," in A. Castañeda Castro (ed.) *Enseñanza de gramática avanzada de ELE: criterios y recursos*. Madrid: SGEL, pp. 9–38.

Alonso-Aparicio, I. and Llopis-García, R. (2019) "La didáctica de la oposición imperfecto/perfecto simple desde una perspectiva cognitiva," in Ibarretxe-Antuñano, I., Cadierno, T., and Castro, A. C., (eds.) *Lingüística cognitiva y español LE/L2*. New York: Routledge, pp. 274–299. https://doi.org/10.4324/9781315622842-13.

Alonso-Raya, R., Castañeda Castro, A., Martinez-Gila, P., et al. (2021) *Gramática basica del estudiante de español: A1-B2 (Nueva edición revisada)*. Barcelona: Difusión.

Aristu, A. (2020) *Cómo aprender léxico con el mapeado de textos*, Campamento Norte. https://campamentonorte.com/como-aprender-lexico-con-el-mapeado-de-textos/.

Aristu, A. and Ríos, L. T. (2021) "El mapeado de textos: un recurso para el aprendizaje del léxico," *marcoELE. Revista de Didáctica Español Lengua Extranjera*, (33), pp. 1–18.

Arnett, C., Suñer, F., and Pust, D. (2019) "Using cooperation scripts and animations to teach grammar in the foreign language classroom," *Yearbook of the German Cognitive Linguistics Association*, 7(1), pp. 31–50. https://doi.org/10.1515/gcla-2019-0003.

Arnett, C. and Suñer, F. (2019) "Leveraging cognitive linguistic approaches to grammar teaching with multimedia animations," *Journal of Cognitive Science*, 20(3), pp. 365–399. https://doi.org/10.17791/JCS.2019.20.3.365.

Azuma, M. and Littlemore, J. (2010) "Promoting creativity in English language classrooms," *JACET Kansai Journal*, 12, pp. 8–19.

Bachman, L. F. (1990) *Fundamental Considerations in Language Testing*. Oxford: Oxford University Press.

Barkley, E. F., Major, C. H., and Cross, K. P. (2014) *Collaborative Learning Techniques: A Handbook for College Faculty*. San Francisco: Wiley.

Benati, A. and Lee, J. F. (eds.) (2015) "Special Issue: Processing instruction: New insights after twenty years of theory, research and application," *International Review of Applied Linguistics in Language Teaching*, 53(2). https://doi.org/10.1515/iral-2015-frontmatter2.

Benati, A. and Nuzzo, E. (2017) "Editorial," *Instructed Second Language Acquisition*, 1(1), pp. 1–4. https://doi.org/10.1558/isla.33325.

Bielak, J. and Pawlak, M. (2011) "Teaching English tense and aspect with the help of cognitive grammar: An empirical study," Studies in Second Language Learning and Teaching, 1(3), pp. 365–400. doi:10.14746/ssllt.2011.1.3.4.

Bielak, J. and Pawlak, M. (2013) *Applying Cognitive Grammar in the Foreign Language Classroom*. Berlin, Heidelberg: Springer. https://doi.org/10.1007/978-3-642-27455-8.

Boas, H. C. (ed.) (2022) *Directions for Pedagogical Construction Grammar: Learning and Teaching (with) Constructions*. Berlin: De Gruyter. https://doi.org/10.1515/9783110746723.

Boers, F. (2011) "Cognitive semantic ways of teaching figurative phrases: An assessment," *Review of Cognitive Linguistics*, 9(1), pp. 227–261. https://doi.org/10.1075/rcl.9.1.11boe.

Boers, F. (2013) "Cognitive linguistic approaches to teaching vocabulary: Assessment and integration," *Language Teaching*, 46(2), pp. 208–224. https://doi.org/10.1017/S0261444811000450.

Boers, F., De Rycker, A., and De Knop, S. (2010) "Fostering language teaching efficiency through cognitive linguistics: Introduction," in S. De Knop, F. Boers, and A. De Rycker (eds.) *Fostering Language Teaching Efficiency through Cognitive Linguistics*. Berlin: De Gruyter Mouton, pp. 1–26. https://doi.org/10.1515/9783110245837.1.

Boers, F. and Demecheleer, M. (1998) "A cognitive semantic approach to teaching prepositions," *English Language Teaching Journal*, 53, pp. 197–204.

Boers, F. and Lindstromberg, S. (2008) *Cognitive Linguistic Approaches to Teaching Vocabulary and Phraseology*. Berlin: Mouton de Gruyter.

Boers, F. and Lindstromberg, S. (2009) *Optimizing a Lexical Approach to Instructed Second Language Acquisition*. London: Palgrave Macmillan. https://doi.org/10.1057/9780230245006.

Cadierno, T. (2008a) "Learning to talk about motion in a foreign language," in P. Robinson and N. C. Ellis (eds.) *Handbook of Cognitive Linguistics and Second Language Acquisition*. New York: Routledge, pp. 239–275.

Cadierno, T. (2008b) "Motion events in Danish and Spanish: A focus on form pedagogical approach," in S. De Knop and A. De Rycker (eds.) *Cognitive Approaches to Pedagogical Grammar*. New York: Mouton de Gruyter, pp. 259–294.

Canale, M. and Swain, M. (1980) "Theoretical bases of communicative approaches to second language teaching and testing," *Applied Linguistics*, I(1), pp. 1–47. https://doi.org/10.1093/applin/I.1.1.

Castañeda Castro, A. (2012) "Perspective and meaning in pedagogical descriptions of Spanish as a foreign language," in G. Ruiz-Fajardo (ed.) *Methodological Developments in Teaching Spanish as a Second and Foreign Language*. Newcastle upon Tyne: Cambridge Scholars, pp. 221–272.

Castañeda Castro, A. and Alhmoud, Z. (2014) "Una aproximación al sistema verbal aplicable a la enseñanza de ELE," in A. Castañeda Castro (ed.)

Enseñanza de gramática avanzada de ELE: criterios y recursos. Madrid: SGEL, pp. 267–294.

Cenoz Iragui, J. (2004) "El concepto de competencia comunicativa," in J. Sánchez Lobato J. and Santos Gargallo, I. (eds.) *Vademécum para la formación de profesores. Enseñar español como segunda lengua/lengua extranjera*. Madrid: SGEL, pp. 449–465.

Colasacco, M. (2019) "A cognitive approach to teaching deictic motion verbs to German and Italian students of Spanish," *International Review of Applied Linguistics in Language Teaching (IRAL)*, 57(1), pp. 71–95. https://doi.org/10.1515/iral-2018-2007.

Conteh, J. (2018) "Translanguaging,", *ELT Journal*, 72(4), pp. 445–447. https://doi.org/10.1093/elt/ccy034.

Contreras, F., Perez Zapatero, J., and Rosales Varo, F. (2019) *Proyectos*. Barcelona: Difusión.

Dancygier, B. and Vandelanotte, L. (2017) "Internet memes as multimodal constructions," *Cognitive Linguistics*, 28(3), pp. 565–598. https://doi.org/10.1515/cog-2017-0074.

Danesi, M. (1992) "Metaphor and classroom second language learning," *Romance Languages Annual*, 3, pp. 189–194.

Danesi, M. (1993) "Metaphorical competence in second language acquisition and second language teaching," in J.E. Alatis (ed.) *Georgetown University Round Table on Language and Linguistics*. Washington, DC: Georgetown University Press, pp. 489–500.

De Knop, S., Boers, F., and De Rycker, A. (eds.) (2010) *Fostering Language Teaching Efficiency through Cognitive Linguistics*. Berlin: De Gruyter Mouton. https://doi.org/10.1515/9783110245837.

De Knop, S. and Gilquin, G. (eds.) (2016) *Applied Construction Grammar*. Berlin: De Gruyter. https://doi.org/10.1515/9783110458268.

Deignan, A., Gabrys, D., and Solska, A. (1997) "Teaching English metaphors using cross-linguistic awareness-raising activities," *ELT Journal*, 51(4), pp. 352–360. https://doi.org/10.1093/elt/51.4.352.

Dörnyei, Z. (2013) "Communicative language teaching in the 21st century: The 'principled communicative approach,'" in J. Arnold and T. Murphey (eds.) *Meaningful Action: Earl Stevick's Influence on Language Teaching*. Cambridge: Cambridge University Press, pp. 161–171.

Doughty, C.J. and Long, M.H. (eds.) (2003) *The Handbook of Second Language Acquisition*. Oxford: Blackwell Publishing. https://doi.org/10.1002/9780470756492.

Ellis, N.C. (2008) "Usage-based and form-focused language acquisition. The associative learning of constructions, learned attention, and the limited L2 endstate," in P. Robinson and N.C. Ellis (eds.) *Handbook of Cognitive Linguistics and Second Language Acquisition*. New York, NY: Routledge/ Taylor & Francis, pp. 372–405.

Ellis, R. and Shintani, N. (eds.) (2014) *Exploring Language Pedagogy through Second Language Acquisition Research*. New York: Routledge/Taylor & Francis.

Farr, F. and Murray, L. (eds.) (2016) *The Routledge Handbook of Language Learning and Technology*. New York: Routledge/Taylor & Francis.

Forceville, C. (2021) "Multimodality," in X. Wen and J.R. Taylor (eds.) *The Routledge Handbook of Cognitive Linguistics*. New York: Routledge, pp. 676–687.

García Sánchez, C. et al. (2018) *Genial. A1: Nivel A2*. Edited by O. Cruz Moya. Madrid: EnClave-ELE.

Gass, S. and Mackey, A. (eds.) (2012) *The Routledge Handbook of Second Language Acquisition*. London: Routledge.

Gibbs, R.W. (2020) "The Particularities of Metaphorical Experience: An Appreciation of Fiona MacArthur's Metaphor Scholarship," in A.M. Piquer-Píriz and R. Alejo-González (eds.) *Metaphor in Foreign Language Instruction*. Berlin: De Gruyter, pp.17–36. https://doi.org/10.1515/978 3110630367-002.

Gilquin, G. and De Knop, S. (2016) "Exploring L2 constructionist approaches," in S. De Knop and G. Gilquin (eds.) *Applied Construction Grammar*. Berlin: De Gruyter, pp. 3–18. https://doi.org/10.1515/9783110458268-002.

Goldberg, A. (2006) *Constructions at Work*. Oxford: Oxford University Press. https://doi.org/10.1093/acprof:oso/9780199268511.001.0001.

Goldberg, A.E. (1995) *Constructions: A Construction Grammar Approach to Argument Structure*. Chicago: University of Chicago Press.

Goldberg, A.E. (2003) "Constructions: a new theoretical approach to language," *Trends in Cognitive Sciences*, 7(5), pp. 219–224. https://doi.org/ 10.1016/S1364-6613(03)00080-9.

Gonzálvez-García, F. (2019) "Exploring the pedagogical potential of vertical and horizontal relations in the constructicon: The case of the family of subjective-transitive constructions with 'decir' in Spanish," *IRAL* 57(1), pp. 121–145. https://doi.org/10.1515/iral-2018-2009.

Gras, P., Santiago, M., and Polanco, F. (2006) "Tienes que aprendértelos ya, que llevas tres años: los pronombres personales átonos en la clase de E/LE. Un enfoque construccionista," in A. Castillo Carballo et al. (eds.) *Las gramáticas y los diccionarios en la enseñanza del español como segunda lengua: deseo y realidad*, pp. 419–426. https://cvc.cervantes.es/ensenanza/biblioteca_ele/asele/ asele_xv.htm.

Herbst, T. (2016) "Foreign language learning is construction learning – what else? Moving towards pedagogical construction grammar," in S. De Knop and G. Gilquin (eds.) *Applied Construction Grammar*. Berlin: De Gruyter, pp. 21–52. https://doi.org/10.1515/9783110458268-003.

Higueras García, M. (2006) *Las colocaciones y su enseñanza en la clase de ELE*. Madrid: Arco/Libros.

Higueras, M. (2011) Lexical collocations and the learning of Spanish as a foreign language: State of the art and future projects, in Cifuentes Honrubia, J.L., Rodríguez Rosique, S. (Eds.), IVITRA Research in Linguistics and Literature. Amsterdam: John Benjamins Publishing Company, pp. 437–464. https://doi.org/10.1075/ivitra.1.18gar.

Hijazo-Gascón, A. (2021) *Moving Across Languages: Motion Events in Spanish as a Second Language*. Boston: De Gruyter. https://doi.org/10.1515/9783110721072.

Hijazo-Gascón, A. and Llopis-García, R. (2019) "Applied cognitive linguistics and foreign language learning. Introduction to the special issue," *IRAL*, 57(1), pp. 1–20. https://doi.org/10.1515/iral-2018-2004.

Hinkel, E. (ed.) (2005) *Handbook of Research in Second Language Teaching and Learning*. Mahwah, N. J: L. Erlbaum.

Hinkel, E. (2011) *Handbook of Research in Second Language Teaching and Learning*. London: Routledge.

Holme, R. (2010a) "A construction grammar for the classroom," *IRAL* 48(4). https://doi.org/10.1515/iral.2010.015.

Holme, R. (2010b) "Construction grammars: Towards a pedagogical model," *AILA Review*. Edited by J. Littlemore and C. Juchem-Grundmann, 23, pp. 115–133. https://doi.org/10.1075/aila.23.07hol.

Housen, A. and Pierrard, M. (eds) (2005) *Investigations in Instructed Second Language Acquisition*. New York: Mouton de Gruyter. https://doi.org/10.1515/9783110197372.

Ibarretxe-Antuñano, I., Cadierno, T., & Castro, A.C. (2019). Lingüística cognitiva y español LE/L2. New York: Routledge. https://doi.org/10.4324/9781315622842.

Ibarretxe-Antuñano, I. and Cheikh-Khamis, F. (2019) "'How to become a woman without turning into a Barbie': Change-of-state verb constructions and their role in Spanish as a foreign language," *IRAL*, 57(1), pp. 97–120. https://doi.org/10.1515/iral-2018-2008.

Ibarretxe-Antuñano, I. and Hijazo-Gascón, A. (eds.) (2015) *New Horizons in the Study of Motion: Bringing Together Applied and Theoretical Perspectives*. Newcastle upon Tyne: Cambridge Scholars Publishing.

Ibarretxe-Antuñano, I. and Valenzuela, J. (2012). Lingüística cognitiva. Barcelona: Antropos.

Juan-Lázaro, O. and Alejaldre Biel, L. (2020) *Competencias digitales en el aula. Estrategias y modelos de implementación en la enseñanza de idiomas.* enClave-ELE y UDIMA.

Kissling, E. et al. (2018) "Reexamining *por* and *para* in the Spanish foreign language intermediate classroom: A usage-based, cognitive linguistic approach," in A. Tyler, L. Huang, and H. Jan (eds.) *What is Applied Cognitive Linguistics?* Berlin: De Gruyter, pp. 229–256. https://doi.org/10.1515/9783110572186-009.

Kissling, E. and Arnold, T. (2022) "Preliminary evidence that applied cognitive linguistics is effective for novice learners regardless of their individual differences," *Language Teaching Research*, p. 136216882211396. https://doi.org/10.1177/13621688221139626.

Kövecses, Z. (2010) *Metaphor: A Practical Introduction.* Oxford: Oxford University Press.

Kovecses, Z. and Szabco, P. (1996) "Idioms: a view from cognitive semantics," *Applied Linguistics*, 17(3), pp. 326–355. https://doi.org/10.1093/applin/17.3.326.

Kramsch, C. (1998). *Language and Culture.* Oxford: Oxford University Press.

Kramsch, C. (2013) "Culture in foreign language teaching.," *Iranian Journal of Language Teaching Research*, 1(1), pp. 57–78.

Krashen, S. (1985). *The Input Hypothesis: Issues and Implications.* New York: Longman.

Lakoff, G. and Johnson, M. (1980) *Metaphors We Live By.* Chicago: University of Chicago Press.

Lam, Y. (2009) "Applying cognitive linguistics to teaching the Spanish prepositions por and para," *Language Awareness*, 18(1), pp. 2–18. https://doi.org/10.1080/09658410802147345.

Langacker, R.W. (1987) *Foundations of Cognitive Grammar. Vol. 1: Theoretical Prerequisites.* Stanford: Stanford University Press.

Langacker, R.W. (2008) "Cognitive grammar as a basis for language instruction," in P. Robinson and N.C. Ellis (eds.) *Handbook of Cognitive Linguistics and Second Language Acquisition.* New York: Routledge, pp. 66–88.

Langacker, R.W. (2008) "The relevance of cognitive grammar for language pedagogy," in S. De Knop and T. De Rycker (eds.) *Cognitive Approaches to Pedagogical Grammar: A Volume in Honour of René Dirven.* Berlin: De Gruyter Mouton, pp. 7–36. https://doi.org/10.1515/9783110205381.1.7.

Langacker, R.W. (2009) *Investigations in Cognitive Grammar.* New York: Mouton de Gruyter.

Langacker, R.W. (2016) "Working toward a synthesis," *Cognitive Linguistics*, 27(4), pp. 465–477. https://doi.org/10.1515/cog-2016-0004.

Lantolf, J. and Bobrova, L. (2014) "Metaphor instructor in the L2 Spanish classroom: theoretical argument and pedagogical program," Journal of Spanish Language Teaching 1(1), 46–61. doi:10.1080/23247797.2014 .898515.

Larsen-Freeman, D. (2015) "Research into practice: Grammar learning and teaching," *Language Teaching*, 48(2), pp. 263–280. https://doi.org/10.1017/ S0261444814000408.

Lee, D.A. (2001) *Cognitive Linguistics: An Introduction*. Oxford: Oxford University Press.

Lee, J.F. and VanPatten, B. (2003) *Making Communicative Language Teaching Happen*. Boston: McGraw-Hill.

Lewis, M. (1993) *Implementing the Lexical Approach: Putting Theory into Practice*. London: Cengage Learning.

Lewis, M. (1997) *Implementing the Lexical Approach*. London: Language Teaching Publications.

Linder, K.E. (2017) "Fundamentals of hybrid teaching and learning," *New Directions for Teaching and Learning* 149, pp. 11–18. https://doi.org/ 10.1002/tl.20222.

Littlemore, J. (2009) *Applying Cognitive Linguistics to Second Language Learning and Teaching*. London: Palgrave Macmillan

Littlemore, J. (2010) "Metaphoric competence in the first and second language," *CELCR* 13, pp. 293–315.

Littlemore, J. (2011) *Applying Cognitive Linguistics to Second Language Learning and Teaching*. Basingstoke: Palgrave Macmillan.

Littlemore, J. and Juchem-Grundmann, C. (2010) "Introduction to the interplay between cognitive linguistics and second language learning and teaching," *AILA Review*, 23, pp. 1–6. https://doi.org/10.1075/aila.23.01lit.

Littlemore, J. and Low, G. (2006) "Metaphoric Competence, Second Language Learning, and Communicative Language Ability," *Applied Linguistics*, 27(2), pp. 268–294. https://doi.org/10.1093/applin/aml004.

Littlemore, J. and Taylor, J.R. (eds.) (2014) *The Bloomsbury Companion to Cognitive Linguistics*. London: Bloomsbury. https://doi.org/10.5040/ 9781472593689.

Littlewood, W. (2011) "Communicative language teaching: an expanding concept for a changing world," in E. Hinkel (ed.) *Handbook of Research in Second Language Teaching and Learning*. London: Routledge, pp. 559–575.

Llopis-García, R. (2009) *Gramática cognitiva e instrucción de procesamiento para la enseñanza de la selección modal. Un estudio con aprendientes alemanes de español como lengua extranjera.* Unpublished dissertation. Universidad Nebrija.

Llopis-García, R. (2010) "Why cognitive grammar works in the L2 classroom: A case study of mood selection in Spanish," *AILA Review*, 23, pp. 72–94. https://doi.org/10.1075/aila.23.05llo.

Llopis-García, R. (2011) "Cognitive grammar: marking new paths in foreign language teaching," *Verba Hispanica*, 19(1), pp. 111–127. https://doi.org/10.4312/vh.19.1.111-127.

Llopis-García, R. (2015) "Las preposiciones y la metáfora del espacio: aportaciones y potencial de la lingüística cognitiva para su enseñanza," *Journal of Spanish Language Teaching*, 2(1), pp. 51–68. https://doi.org/10.1080/23247797.2015.1042214.

Llopis-García, R. (2016a) "Entrevista con Reyes Llopis en el Canal de ProfeDeELE – Formación profes de español." https://youtu.be/ngkUwCpacdw.

Llopis-García, R. (2016b) "Using cognitive principles in teaching Spanish L2 grammar," *Hesperia: Anuario de filología hispánica*, 19, pp. 29–50.

Llopis-García, R. (2019a) "Gramática cognitiva y selección modal en la enseñanza del español LE/L2," in I. Ibarretxe-Antuñano, T. Cadierno, and A. Castañeda Castro (eds.) *Lingüística cognitiva y español LE/L2*. New York: Routledge/Taylor & Francis, pp. 255–273.

Llopis-García, R. (2019b) "Space, radial networks and prototypes: a cognitive approach to prepositions in Spanish/L2 pedagogy," in. *International Cognitive Linguistics Conference*, Nishinomiya, Japan. https://iclc2019.site.

Llopis-García, R. (Feb. 2020) "Less Can Be More! Re-Thinking Teaching Materials and Dynamics for Small-Sized Classes." *Celebration of Teaching and Learning*, Columbia Center for Teaching and Learning, Columbia University.

Llopis-García, R. (2021a) "No Functions . . . constructions! CxG and cognitive linguistics: powerful allies for user friendly L2 pedagogy," *CogniTextes*, (21). https://doi.org/10.4000/cognitextes.1978.

Llopis-García, R. (2021b) "Plenary: applied cognitive linguistics for meaningful – and successful! – L2 language leaching," in *2nd International Conference for Young Researchers in Cognitive Linguistics*. https://sites.google.com/view/yrcl2021/home.

Llopis-García, R. and Alonso-Aparicio, I. (2018) "Enseñanza de L2 de corte cognitivo: ¿Qué apunta la investigación empírica?," in *11th International Conference of the Spanish Cognitive Linguistics Association (AELCO)*, Universidad de Córdoba. www.uco.es/aelco2018/en/welcome/.

Llopis-García, R. and Alonso-Aparicio, I. (2019) "Cognitive approaches to L2 pedagogy: challenges and shortcomings of empirical testing," in *International Cognitive Linguistics Conference*, Nishinomiya, Japan. https://iclc2019.site.

Llopis-Garcia, R. and Hijazo-Gascón, A. 2019 (eds.) Special Issue: Applied Cognitive Linguistics to L2 acquisition and learning: research and convergence. IRAL 57(1).

Llopis-García, R., Real Espinosa, J.M., and Ruiz Campillo, J.P. (2012) *Qué gramática enseñar, qué gramática aprender*. Madrid: Edinumen.

Long, M.H. and Robinson, P. (1998) "Focus on form: theory, research and practice," in C.J. Doughty and J. Williams (eds.) *Focus on Form in Classroom Second Language Acquisition*. Cambridge: Cambridge University Press, pp. 15–41.

Long, M. (1991) "Focus on form: a design feature in language teaching methodology," in K. de Bot, R.B. Ginsberg, and C. Kramsch (eds.) *Studies in Bilingualism*. Amsterdam: John Benjamins, pp. 39–52. https://doi.org/10.1075/sibil.2.07lon.

Long, M. (2017) "Instructed second language acquisition (ISLA)," *Instructed Second Language Acquisition*, 1(1), pp. 7–44. https://doi.org/10.1558/isla.33314.

Low, G. (2020) "Taking stock after three decades: 'on teaching metaphor' revisited," in A.M. Piquer-Píriz and R. Alejo-González (eds.) *Metaphor in Foreign Language Instruction*. Boston: De Gruyter, pp. 37–56. https://doi.org/10.1515/9783110630367-003.

Luo, H. (2021) "Cognitive Linguistics and Second Language Acquisition," in Xu, W. and Taylor, J. (eds.) *The Routledge Handbook of Cognitive Linguistics*. New York: Routledge, 556–567.

MacArthur, F. (2017) "Using metaphor in the teaching of second/foreign languages," in E. Semino and Z. Demjén (eds.) *The Routledge Handbook of Metaphor and Language*. New York: Routledge, pp. 413–425.

MacArthur, F. and Littlemore, J. (2008) "A discovery approach to figurative language learning with the use of corpora," in F. Boers and S. Lindstromberg (eds.) *Cognitive Linguistic Approaches to Teaching Vocabulary and Phraseology*. New York: Mouton de Gruyter, pp. 159–188. https://doi.org/10.1515/9783110199161.2.159.

Malinowski, D. and Kern, R. (2016) "Limitations and boundaries in language learning and technology," in F. Farr and L. Murray (eds.) *The Routledge Handbook of Language Learning and Technology*. New York: Routledge/Taylor & Francis, pp. 197–209.

Malinowski, D., Maxim, H.H., and Dubreil, S. (2020) *Language Teaching in the Linguistic Landscape: Mobilizing Pedagogy in Public Space*. Cham: Springer.

Martín-Gascón, B., Llopis-García, R., & Alonso-Aparicio, I. (2023) Does L2 assessment make a difference? Testing the empirical validity of applied cognitive linguistics in the acquisition of the Spanish/L2 psych-verb construction. Language Teaching Research, 0(0). https://doi.org/10.1177/13621688231190981.

Masid Blanco, O. (2017) *La metáfora lingüística en español como lengua extranjera (ELE). Estudio pre-experimental en tres niveles de competencia.* Unpublished dissertation. Universidad de Granada.

Méndez Santos, M.C. and Llopis-García, R. (2021) "Implicaciones didácticas sobre los factores cognitivos y afectivos en la enseñanza de ELE," in J.A. Duñabeitia and M. Méndez Santos (eds.) *Factores cognitivos y afectivos en la enseñanza del español como LE/L2*, pp. 259–302. https://doi.org/10.32029/2605-4655.00.03.2021.

Mendo Murillo, S. (2014) "Corporeización y gramática : una propuesta de presentación del contraste por/para en el nivel de usuario básico de E/LE," *redELE 15.*

Mendo Murillo, S. (2019) "El significado de las preposiciones en la enseñanza del español LE/L2: el caso de por y para" in I. Ibarretxe-Antuñano, T. Cadierno, and A. Castañeda Castro (eds.) *Lingüística cognitiva y español LE-L2.* New York: Routledge, pp. 220–234.

Mompean, J.A. and Mompean-Guillamón, P. (2012) "La fonología cognitiva," in I. Ibarretxe-Antuñano and J. Valenzuela (eds.) *Lingüística Cognitiva.* Barcelona: Anthropos, pp. 307–326.

Muñoz, R.A. and Suárez-Campos, L. (2019) "El desarrollo de la competencia metafórica en la enseñanza del español LE/L2," in I. Ibarretxe-Antuñano, T. Cadierno, and A. Castañeda Castro (eds.) *Lingüística cognitiva y español LE/L2.* New York: Routledge, pp. 371–391.

Nacey, S. (2017) "Metaphor comprehension and production in a second language," in E. Semino and Z. Demjén (eds.) *The Routledge Handbook of Metaphor and Language*, pp. 503–516.

Nassaji, H. (2016) "Research timeline: form-focused instruction and second language acquisition," *Language Teaching*, 49(1), pp. 35–62. https://doi.org/10.1017/S0261444815000403.

Niemeier, S. (2013) A cognitive grammar perspective on tense and aspect. In: Salaberry, M. and Comajoan, L. (eds.) *Research Design and Methodology in Studies on L2 Tense and Aspect.* Boston: De Gruyter Mouton, pp. 11–56. https://doi.org/10.1515/9781934078167.11

Niemeier, S. (2017) "Teaching (in) metaphors," in F. Ervas, E. Gola, and M. G. Rossi (eds.) *Metaphor in Communication, Science and Education.* Berlin: De Gruyter, pp. 267–282. https://doi.org/10.1515/9783110549928-015.

Pan, M.X. (2019) "The effectiveness of the conceptual metaphor approach to English idiom acquisition by young Chinese learners," *Metaphor and the Social World*, 9(1), pp. 59–82. https://doi.org/10.1075/msw.17024.pan.

Pascual Rocha, P. (May 2016) "Un poquito más de luz sobre las preposiciones," *SonoraELE. Online Spanish School*.https://sonoraele.com/un-poquito-mas-de-luz-sobre-las-preposiciones/.

Pérez Serrano, M. (2017) *La enseñanza-aprendizaje del vocabulario en ELE desde los enfoques léxicos*. Madrid: Arco/Libros.

Pérez Serrano, M. (2018) "Which type of instruction fosters chunk learning? Preliminary conclusions," *Revista de Lingüística y Lenguas Aplicadas*, 13(1), p. 133. https://doi.org/10.4995/rlyla.2018.7886.

Pérez Sobrino, P. (2017) *Multimodal Metaphor and Metonymy in Advertising*. Amsterdam: John Benjamins. https://doi.org/10.1075/ftl.2.

Philip, G. (2011) *Colouring Meaning: Collocation and Connotation in Figurative Language*. Amsterdam: John Benjamins. https://doi.org/10.1075/scl.43.

Piquer-Píriz, A.M. and Alejo-González, R. (eds.) (2019) *Metaphor in Foreign Language Instruction*. Berlin: De Gruyter. https://doi.org/10.1515/9783110630367.

Piquer-Píriz, A.M. and Boers, F. (2019) "La lingüística cognitiva y sus aplicaciones a la enseñanza de lenguas extranjeras," in I. Ibarretxe-Antuñano, T. Cadierno, and A. Castañeda Castro (eds.) *Lingüística cognitiva y español LE/L2*. New York: Routledge, pp. 52–70.

Pütz, M., Niemeier, S., and Dirven, R. (eds.) (2001a) *Applied Cognitive Linguistics, I, Theory and Language Acquisition*. Boston: De Gruyter Mouton. https://doi.org/10.1515/9783110866247.

Pütz, M., Niemeier, S., and Dirven, R. (eds.) (2001b) *Applied Cognitive Linguistics, II, Language Pedagogy*. Boston: De Gruyter Mouton. https://doi.org/10.1515/9783110866254.

Robinson, P.J. and Ellis, N.C. (eds.) (2008) *Handbook of Cognitive Linguistics and Second Language Acquisition*. New York: Routledge.

Rocca, S. (2018) "Introducing the special issue: MOBILizing language learning in the 21st Century," *Languages*, 3(1), pp. 1–3. https://doi.org/10.3390/languages3010002.

Román-Mendoza, E. (2018) *Aprender a aprender en la era digital: tecnopedagogía crítica para la enseñanza del español LE/L2*. New York: Routledge.

Rufat, A.S. (2015) "Enseñanza de gramática avanzada de ELE. Criterios y recursos," *Journal of Spanish Language Teaching*, 2(1), pp. 96–98. https://doi.org/10.1080/23247797.2015.1019306.

Ruiz, V. (2022) "Una imagen vale más que mil reglas: Gramática visual en el aula de ELE." Online presentation. Instituto Cervantes de Praga, 18 February.

Ruiz, V. and Torres Ríos, L. (2022) "Perspectiva para enseñar el contraste de pretérito e imperfecto." https://campamentonorte.com/cursos/como-ensenar-gramatica/.

Ruiz de Mendoza Ibáñez, F. and Llach, M.P. (2016) "Cognitive pedagogical grammar and meaning construction in L2," in S. De Knop and G. Gilquin (eds.) *Applied Construction Grammar*. Berlin: De Gruyter, pp. 151–184. https://doi.org/10.1515/9783110458268-007.

Sans Baulenas, N., Martín Peris, E., Garmendia, A., Conejo, E., and Garrido, P. (2017) *Bitácora: curso de español. 3, Libro del alumno B1*. Stuttgart: Klett.

Schmitt, N. (2008) "Instructed second language vocabulary learning," *Language Teaching Research*, 12(3), pp. 329–363. https://doi.org/10.1177/1362168808089921.

Segura Munguía, S. (2014) *Diccionario etimológico de Medicina*. Universidad de Deusto.

Slobin, D. (1996) "From 'thought and language' to 'thinking for speaking'." In Gumperz, J.J. and Levinson, S.C. (eds.) *Rethinking Linguistic Relativity*. Cambridge: Cambridge University Press, 70–96.

Soriano, C. (2012) "La metáfora conceptual," in I. Ibarretxe-Antuñano and J. Valenzuela (eds.) *Lingüística cognitiva*. Barcelona: Anthropos, pp. 97–122.

Suárez Campos, L.G. (2020) *La conceptualización metafórica y metonímica de la IRA en búlgaro y español y su adquisición en español LE/L2*. Unpublished dissertation. Universidad de Zaragoza.

Suárez-Campos, L., Hijazo-Gascón, A., and Ibarretxe-Antuñano, I. (2020) "Metaphor and Spanish as a Foreign Language," in A.M. Piquer-Píriz and R. Alejo-González (eds.) *Metaphor in Foreign Language Instruction*. Boston: De Gruyter Mouton, pp. 79–98. https://doi.org/10.1515/9783110630367-005.

Suñer, F. and Roche, J. (2019) "Embodiment in concept-based L2 grammar teaching: The case of German light verb constructions," *IRAL* 59(3), pp. 421–447. https://doi.org/10.1515/iral-2018-0362.

Talmy, L. (2000) *Toward a Cognitive Semantics*. Cambridge, MA: MIT Press.

Tay, D. (2014) "Lakoff and the Theory of Conceptual Metaphor," in J. Littlemore and J.R. Taylor (eds.) *The Bloomsbury Companion to Cognitive Linguistics*. New York: Bloomsbury, pp. 49–59.

Taylor, J.R. (2008) "Prototypes in cognitive linguistics," in P. Robinson and N.C. Ellis (eds.) *Handbook of Cognitive Linguistics and Second Language Acquisition*. New York: Routledge, pp. 49–75.

Taylor, J.R. and Littlemore, J. (2014) "Introduction," in J. Littlemore and J.R. Taylor (eds.) *The Bloomsbury Companion to Cognitive Linguistics*. New York: Bloomsbury, pp. 1–26.

Toth, P.D. and Davin, K.J. (2016) "The sociocognitive imperative of L2 pedagogy," *The Modern Language Journal*, 100(S1), pp. 148–168. https://doi.org/10.1111/modl.12306.

Troitiño, S. (2017) 'Implicaciones de crear materiales desde una perspectiva léxica', in F. Herrera (ed.) *Enseñar léxico en el aula de español: el poder de las palabras*. Barcelona: Difusión, pp. 143–162.

Tyler, A. (2008) "Cognitive linguistics and second language instruction," in P. Robinson and N.C. Ellis (eds.) *Handbook of Cognitive Linguistics and Second Language Acquisition*. New York: Routledge, pp. 456–488.

Tyler, A. (2012) *Cognitive Linguistics and Second Language Learning*. New York: Routledge. https://doi.org/10.4324/9780203876039.

Tyler, A. and Evans, V. (2003) *The Semantics of English Prepositions: Spatial Scenes, Embodied Meaning, and Cognition*. Cambridge: Cambridge University Press. https://doi.org/10.1017/CBO9780511486517.

Tyler, A. and Evans, V. (2004) "Applying cognitive linguistics to pedagogical grammar: the case of over," in M. Achard and S. Niemeier (eds.) *Cognitive Linguistics, Second Language Acquisition, and Foreign Language Teaching*. New York: Mouton de Gruyter, pp. 257–280. https://doi.org/10.1515/9783110199857.257.

Tyler, A. and Huang, L. (2018) "Introduction," in A. Tyler, L. Huang, and H. Jan (eds.) *What Is Applied Cognitive Linguistics?* Berlin: De Gruyter, pp. 1–34. https://doi.org/10.1515/9783110572186-001.

Tyler, A., Huang, L., and Jan, H. (eds) (2018) *What Is Applied Cognitive Linguistics?: Answers From Current SLA Research*. Berlin: De Gruyter. https://doi.org/10.1515/9783110572186.

Tyler, A., Mueller, C., and Ho, V. (2011) "Applying cognitive linguistics to learning the semantics of English *to, for* and *at*: an experimental investigation.," *VIAL* 8, pp. 180–205.

Tyler, A., Mueller, C.M., and Ho, V. (2010) "Applying cognitive linguistics to instructed L2 learning: the English modals," *AILA Review*, 23, pp. 30–49. https://doi.org/10.1075/aila.23.03tyl.

VanPatten, B. (1996) *Input Processing and Grammar Instruction in Second Language Acquisition*. Norwood, NJ: Ablex.

VanPatten, B. (ed.) (2004) *Processing Instruction: Theory, Research, and Commentary*. London: Routledge.

VanPatten, B. (2015) "Foundations of processing instruction," *IRAL* 53(2). https://doi.org/10.1515/iral-2015-0005.

VanPatten, B., Leeser, M.J., and Keating, G.D. (2012) *Sol y viento: beginning Spanish*. New York: McGraw-Hill.

Verspoor, M. and Lowie, W. (2003) "Making sense of polysemous words," *Language Learning*, 53(3), pp. 547–586.

Young, R. (2011) "Interactional competence in language learning, teaching, and testing," in E. Hinkel (ed.) *Handbook of Research in Second Language Teaching and Learning*. New York: Routledge, pp. 444–461.

Zhao, H. et al. (2018) "Polysemy and conceptual metaphors: a cognitive linguistics approach to vocabulary learning," in A. Tyler, L. Huang, and H. Jan (eds.) *What is Applied Cognitive Linguistics?* Berlin: De Gruyter, pp. 257–286. https://doi.org/10.1515/9783110572186-010.

Acknowledgements

This work is dedicated to my family: my parents Cristina and José Antonio, my husband Chris, and our dog Frida. Without your love, care, and support nothing would be possible. Also to my cheer squad: dear friends all over the world who have encouraged and celebrated every step of this *Element*, and of my career in general.

I would like to thank Nick Riches and Sarah Duffy, the editors of the Series, for including me in this project and for all the invaluable input they have offered from the start.

And to any and all readers: here's hoping this work encourages you to bring cognitive linguistics into your L2 classroom! ✦

Cognitive Linguistics

Sarah Duffy
Northumbria University

Sarah Duffy is Senior Lecturer in English Language and Linguistics at Northumbria University. She has published primarily on metaphor interpretation and understanding, and her forthcoming monograph for Cambridge University Press (co-authored with Michele Feist) explores *Time, Metaphor, and Language* from a cognitive science perspective. Sarah is Review Editor of the journal, *Language and Cognition*, and Vice President of the UK Cognitive Linguistics Association.

Nick Riches
Newcastle University

Nick Riches is a Senior Lecturer in Speech and Language Pathology at Newcastle University. His work has investigated language and cognitive processes in children and adolescents with autism and developmental language disorders, and he is particularly interested in usage-based accounts of these populations.

About the Series
Cambridge Elements in Cognitive Linguistics aims to extend the theoretical and methodological boundaries of cognitive linguistics. It will advance and develop established areas of research in the discipline, as well as address areas where it has not traditionally been explored and areas where it has yet to become well-established.

Cambridge Elements

Cognitive Linguistics

Printed in the United States
by Baker & Taylor Publisher Services